the Purse-uit
of Holiness

the Purse-uit of Holiness

Learning to Imitate the Master Designer

Rhonda Rhea

a division of Baker Publishing Group
Grand Rapids, Michigan

Published by Revell
a division of Baker Publishing Group
P.O. Box 6287, Grand Rapids, MI 49516-6287
www.revellbooks.com

Printed in the United States of America

Library of Congress Cataloging-in-Publication Data

Rhea, Rhonda.
The purse-uit of holiness : learning to imitate the master designer / Rhonda Rhea.
p. cm.
Includes bibliographical references.
ISBN 978-0-8007-3253-0 (pbk.)
1. Christian women—Religious life. 2. Holiness. 3. Handbags—Anecdotes. I. Title.
II. Title: Pursuit of holiness.
BV4527.R485 2008
248.8′43—dc22 2008011234

Portions of select chapters in the book are adapted from the author's columns in *St. Louis Metro Voice*, *Inspire* magazine (St. Louis), "Sermon Illustrator" and "Daily Wisdom" online devotionals, and from the author's blog.

In keeping with biblical principles of creation stewardship, Baker Publishing Group advocates the responsible use of our natural resources. As a member of the Green Press Initiative, our company uses recycled paper when possible. The text paper of this book is comprised of 30% post-consumer waste.

In loving memory of Lucile Harrell,
a wonderful grandma who tutored me
in the relentless shopping pursuit of a purse
that could be pretty and practical at the same time,
and who tutored me in the uncompromising pursuit
of laughing and living well at the same time.

Contents

Acknowledgments

I'm thoroughly convinced there's no way I could complete a book project of any consequence without my husband, counselor, hero, pastor, supporter, encourager: Richie Rhea. He teaches me more and more each day about the life of holiness as I watch him live it out. And that holy life truly does look mah-velous on my honey!

Other supports in the Rhea System? My college boys, ministers and musicians, Andrew Rhea and Jordan Rhea; my writing partner and proofreader, Kaley Rhea; and my sweet encouragers, Allie Rhea and Daniel Rhea. All along the way, the laughs my kids inspire are hysterically therapeutic—and some of them make great material.

How do I love my prayer team? Let me count the ways! There's no way to overvalue the prayer investment of my amazing team of prayer warriors. Undergirding every point of this project and others from start to finish and beyond, their investment is absolutely inestimable. My humble and sincere thanks to Janet Bridgeforth, Tina Byus, Diane Campbell, Mary Clark, Theresa Easterday, Chris Hendrickson, Melinda Massey, and Peanuts Rudolph.

Super Agent Pamela Harty continues to leap tall buildings in a single bound. Big thanks to Pamela and all those at The Knight

Agency who put such muscle and heart into their work to make it possible for me to do what I do.

I so appreciate my marvelous editor, Jennifer Leep, and the spectacular team at the Revell division of Baker Publishing Group. From the crack editorial team to the talented art department and the creative marketing and publicity crews, every person has made the process a joy—all while sharing my heart for a fun and fruitful project that will inspire a giggle and bless the hearts of readers and—most importantly—bless the heart of God.

More thanks to my church family at Troy First Baptist Church for prayers and encouragement and for seeing every part of my ministry as an extension of our church's ministry. And another nod of thanks to Halo & Wings, our local Christian book store here in Troy, Missouri.

Additional thank-yous to the Advanced Writers and Speakers Association for sharing knowledge, for praying, and for listening with hardly an eyeroll when I whine—along with sincere thanks to my good friend, ministry counselor, web designer, and marketing guru, Joanne Sampl of Next-Step-Up Communications.

High-calorie thanks to Cappuccino's Café in O'Fallon, Missouri, for being my "home office away from home office" while pounding out the last few chapters. I found that one Venti Mocha is good for at least two chapters (though since it's made with espresso, some of the chapters are all one sentence). The yumalicious double fudge cake made this the most fattening book I've ever written. But I finished with a double fudge smile.

Ever and always, my biggest thanks is reserved for my high and holy heavenly Father. Worthy to write a book with "holiness" anywhere in the title? I'm not even close. Yet I believe he loves to prove that he truly can use *anyone.* All my thanks and praise to the holy, holy, holy God who makes this journey oh so heavenly.

Therefore, prepare your minds for action; be self-controlled; set your hope fully on the grace to be given you when Jesus Christ is revealed. As obedient children, do not conform to the evil desires you had when you lived in ignorance. But just as he who called you is holy, so be holy in all you do; for it is written: "Be holy, because I am holy."

1 Peter 1:13-16

Introduction: It's in the Bag!

"Prepare your minds for action . . ."

Does anyone else remember those Felix the Cat cartoons? Whatever happened to Felix?

I can still sing the song: "Felix the Cat. The wonderful, wonderful cat. Whenever he gets in a fix, he reaches into his bag of tricks." It was always such fun wondering what weird wonder Felix was going to pop out of his bag next. Felix was the MacGyver of cartoon cats.

Of course, I have a bag something like Felix's. My purse is a regular bag of tricks. Sometimes I find things in there I didn't even know I had. Was that popcorn I noticed in there the other day? A handful of Cheesy Doodles from last summer maybe? A Junior Mint (and it'll be perfectly fine after I pick the lint off, I'm sure)? Throw in a checkered tablecloth and a couple of soft drinks and I could practically serve a picnic lunch right out of my purse. Spur of the moment meal? It's in the bag! I wonder if even Felix could do that.

Magic MacGyver Moments

With my magic bag in tow, I love it when I get to stretch my MacGyver purse-muscle. A girlfriend has an unspeakable nail disaster—and she has a French manicure! Never fear. Rhea-Gyver is here. I feel a little like an action/adventure hero as I cleverly and clandestinely pull out the Wite-Out for the tip touch-up, dig out a little bottle of varnish for a clear topcoat, and totally save the nail day. Talk about being prepared for action!

But we have a much greater need to be prepared for non-manicure-related action. One version of our focal 1 Peter 1:13–16 passage begins with the instruction to "think clearly" (NLT[b]). Clear thinking is about more than the clear make-do polish from the magic bag. When we're thinking clearly spiritually, we understand how vital to life a passionate pursuit of holiness is. We need to have a thorough and accurate perception of where our pursuit of holiness should lead us. We really must think clearly.

But to be perfectly honest, the topic of holiness has sometimes been a bit of a cloudy little mystery in my mind. Psalm 99:9 says, "The LORD our God is holy." His holiness means that he is set apart. He's not like me; he is completely perfect, without even a hint of sin. The Word of God makes it quite clear that the Lord and only the Lord is holy.

Then, right in the middle of that clear thinking, I find verse 16 of 1 Peter 1: "You must be holy because I am holy" (NLT[b]). What can I possibly pull out of my magic bag to give me the ability to obey this command? I still struggle with the flesh. I still live in a sin-cursed world. I have faults and shortcomings and all kinds of weaknesses. I still sin.

Thankfully, in one sense, that holiness is already mine. Yours, too, if you've surrendered your life to Jesus. Not because of anything holy we've done, but exclusively by the work of Christ on our behalf. He makes us blameless by his death on the cross. Hebrews 9:14–15 says, "How much more, then, will the blood of Christ, who through the eternal Spirit offered himself unblemished to God, cleanse our consciences from acts that lead to death, so that we may serve the living God! For this reason Christ is the mediator of a new covenant, that those who are called may receive the promised eternal inheritance—now that he has died as a ransom to set them free from the sins committed under the first covenant."

Holiness becomes a perfectly accurate description of our condition because of the righteousness we can now borrow straight from Christ. He gives us his own perfection; and he's the one who sets us apart. Sounds magical, but it's nothing like the bag. No, it's so much better!

In that sense, we are his holy people. In another sense, he instructs us to be growing in righteousness—becoming more and more holy in the way we live.

Clear or Partly Cloudy?

The Father doesn't want us to have a cloudy kind of thinking. "Prepare your minds for action" is also translated to "gird up the loins of your mind" (NKJV). To gird up the loins was to gather the bulky robes so a person could move ahead without getting all tripped up (if only he'd had a large purse). He could get there more quickly and in better order without the hindrances.

We need to get rid of any hindrances to clear thinking. Let's get our minds in gear for holiness. We're called not only to get our minds in gear, but we're clearly called to "action." Let's get ourselves ready for hot pursuit. Girdle up and get going!

When I'm action-ready and thinking clearly, it becomes clearer that personal holiness is as much about the pursuit as the arrival. We're supposed to grow in holiness. Action! 1 Thessalonians 4:1 makes that plain: "Finally, brothers, we instructed you how to live in order to please God, as in fact you are living. Now we ask you and urge you in the Lord Jesus to do this more and more." Growing "more and more" in righteous, holy living! Verse 7 in the same chapter of 1 Thessalonians says, "For God did not call us to be impure, but to live a holy life." And that holy life isn't merely a nice direction to grow. It's a calling.

Calling All Pursuers

Thank you, friend, for setting out on the *Purse-uit of Holiness* with me. I'm thrilled we can respond to the call together! And I'm thrilled we can do it with plenty of chuckles along the way. Hopefully, just as it says in the "Felix the Cat" song, "You'll laugh so hard, your sides will ache, your heart will go pitter-pat."

But I have to tell you, it's my deep desire that this be not merely a funny book. Not even just a look at holiness. But a genuine *pursuit*. Chasing down holiness and making it ours.

Let's pursue the holiness calling with everything we've got. Preparing for action and thinking clearly, we can begin to understand that holiness comes as we depend on the filling of the Holy Spirit and as we find out how to surrender more and more to his perfect will with more complete abandon. As that happens, I think we'll see the holiness we're pursuing is *in the bag!*

Heavenly Father, thank you for your divine power that gives us absolutely everything we need for life and godliness. Take us to glorious places of a richer, holy life. Challenge us to pursue you and to pursue that holy life with everything we have—inside and outside the purse. Let us know you more fully, love you more deeply, serve you more genuinely, and follow you more closely. May you find us in the holiest places with you, and may we honor you completely. All glory and honor to you!

Thank you for the gift of your Word. Thank you that when we really look at it and study it and make it a part of our lives, we're never, never the same. Let us walk away from this holy pursuit changed because of your loving work in our hearts as we look at the truths you've so graciously given us in your Word.

Thank you, Father, that you invented laughter. Thank you for calling us to a life of adventure and a life of great fun! I love to think of how you love our pleasure. Thank you! I pray that you will fill our pursuit of holiness with laughter and joy—the kind that will make you smile too.

I pray for the one reading right now. If she needs encouragement, I pray she will be lifted up. If she needs discipline, I pray you'll grant it. If she needs joy, I ask that you please give it to her in big, falling-over doses—in the biggest, best way. If she has any need at all, I pray you will meet her exactly where she is, that you will meet even her most personal needs. If one of those needs is a need to make a change, I pray she'll be confronted by your Word and in your most gracious love. Give her reminders of that extravagant, unconditional, glorious love you have for her all along the way.

Oh Lord, lead us in passionate pursuit—in your most glorious "action adventure." Take us to heavenly, holy places with you!

Part 1

"Be self-controlled"

1 A Walk-in Purse

Self-control can be slippery. For instance, really and truly, who can exercise complete closet self-control when there's one of those "75% off, major clearance, we'll-practically-pay-you-to-take-this-great-stuff" kinds of sales? And when you consider the need for a purse in every color to make the perfect combo with every cute pair of shoes in the closet, it becomes clear. This is going to take a lot of purses. And more closet space.

A Walk-in Purse

I have a walk-in closet that got so over-pursed I couldn't walk in anymore. I could squeeze in a toe, maybe a toe and a half, and that was it. Never mind that I have enough purses to fill an 18-wheeler (and more accurately, I think I could fill an 18-wheeler with 16 wheels tied behind my back).

I finally rearranged the closet just enough to get both feet in. Ah, a walk-in again. Sort of. Oh well. You know . . . baby steps.

Baby steps are still about all I can take in there. But it's exciting to be able to get most of my body inside the closet once more. It's downright inspiring. It's amazing what a couple of shelves will do.

Since it's all purse-related, it hit me around closet clean-up time: I could honestly use a major rearranging in this purse I'm carrying! How about a walk-in purse? My handbag is at least as cramped as the worst closet. I couldn't get a toe in this thing if I tried (not that I can think of a single reason to try to squeeze a toe in my purse). Maybe my purse could use some shelves.

My husband thought the walk-in purse idea was totally ridiculous. He suggested something closer to putting a shoulder strap on a semi. *Breaker, breaker, good buddy, the 18-wheeler is back.* After considering it, I decided his idea wasn't half bad. Hmm, if the idea is not half bad, would that make it "*semi*-good"?

Self-control vs. Shelf-control

When it comes to holiness, though, "semi-good" is just not good enough. Why should we settle? Our heavenly Father has called us to something so much higher. I'm not talking about a higher shelf here. I'm talking about the call to live by a higher standard—his call and his standard. What an honor to receive that calling from our holy God! Second Peter 1:3 says, "As we know Jesus better, his divine power gives us everything we need for living a godly life. He has called us to receive his own glory and goodness!" (NLT[a]). He has called us.

Oh Lord, let us know you better! According to this verse, as we know him better, we have more power for living the godly life he has called us to live. We have the immense power of our omnipotent God to give us everything we need for holy living. And take a look at verse 6 in the same chapter: "Knowing God leads to self-control. Self-control leads to patient endurance, and patient endurance leads to godliness" (NLT[a]).

Without self-control, there will be no holy life. Proverbs 25:28 says, "A person without self-control is as defenseless as a city with broken-down walls" (NLT[a]). So much worse than a closet without a single shelf. We find the power for self-control in knowing God. Look again at how verse 6 makes it oh so plain: "Knowing God leads to self-control." The glory and goodness he wants to put on display in our lives comes straight from him.

Self-control is part of the fruit of the Spirit. And he's not known as the Really Good Spirit. He is the HOLY Spirit. Holy, holy, holy. And it's his filling that brings holiness into our lives. We will have exactly as much of his holiness as we have of his indwelling presence controlling our thoughts and actions.

Room to Grow?

Maybe you don't have a lot of room in your closet either. Maybe there's no room for anything new in your purse. But do you have room to grow in living a life of holiness? In all honesty, who doesn't?

We can start by making a realistic evaluation of ourselves. It's easy to get puffed up—to think that if we haven't murdered, dabbled in the occult, or stolen any handbags, we've got it pretty much together. But there's victory in realizing we have room to grow. Getting rid of pride and emptying ourselves is a great step of growth in itself. Proverbs 3:7 says, "Do not be wise in your own eyes."

When I'm puffed up and full of myself, how can I be full of a holy God? Full of him or full of me—I get to choose. Where does ego fit into the life of holiness? Nowhere. Giving up a focus on self-importance sounds difficult. But I can guarantee you, you will never, ever look back with even the tiniest regret on any decision you make to shove ego over and give Jesus first place.

So let's get going on our pursuit of holiness by asking the Father to build more self-control into our lives—the kind of self-control that inspires Spirit-control. Let's let go of self and latch on to him.

That truly is inspiring. Even more inspiring than a purse so neat that you have room to spare.

> So I say, live by the Spirit, and you will not gratify the desires of the sinful nature. For the sinful nature desires what is contrary to the Spirit, and the Spirit what is contrary to the sinful nature. They are in conflict with each other, so that you do not do what you want. But if you are led by the Spirit, you are not under law. The acts of the sinful nature are obvious: sexual immorality, impurity and debauchery; idolatry and witchcraft; hatred, discord, jealousy, fits of rage, selfish ambition, dissensions, factions and envy; drunkenness, orgies, and the like. I warn you, as I did before, that those who live like this will not inherit the kingdom of God. But the fruit of the Spirit is love, joy, peace, patience, kindness, goodness, faithfulness, gentleness and self-control. Against such things there is no law. Those who belong to Christ Jesus have crucified the sinful nature with its passions and desires. Since we live by the Spirit, let us keep in step with the Spirit. Let us not become conceited, provoking and envying each other.
>
> Galatians 5:16–26

---

2 Pocketbook Power

Isn't purse shopping sort of aerobic? If you can keep a pretty good clip going at the mall, I think you can earn at least an aerobic point or two. That means the right kind of purse shopping has the potential power to get you into shape. Now that's pocketbook power. And I do know that the right sale price can raise my heart rate and leave me breathing heavier than any old ordinary exercise routine.

Of course, I'm getting a little more lax all the time in my definition of "exercise routine." Walking to the end of the driveway to get the mail? Exercise routine. Bending over to take my shoes off? Exercise. And that takes care of the abs workout. Making coffee? That's burning calories. The coffee is on one of the high shelves. That means there's stretching involved. If I turn on the music and make coffee to the beat, I think that officially classifies it as exercise. "And one. And two. And scoop. And perk."

Squirming into my tightest jeans? Now there's some significant sweating. Eventually, I'll be able to bend after I zip 'em.

Exercising a Reality Check

Sooner or later, exercise reality does catch up with me. I usually get my most intense reality jolt as summer is approaching and I know I'm going to have to shop for more than a purse. When it's time to start the summer shopping, those four little syllables that strike fear into the heart of a woman can scare me right onto the treadmill. The four syllables? *Swim-suit-shop-ping.*

The last time I had to do the swimsuit shopping thing, I went to a shop that had a gazillion black Lycra-spandexed suits to choose from. Black, not because I was going for a Goth kind of look or anything. No, it was because black is supposed to make me look at least five pounds thinner—without even having to take an extra lap around the mailbox.

I found myself in the dressing room with forty-seven variations on the stretchy black swimsuit. The first one looked sturdy. Sturdy is good, right? I pulled it out and worked my way in, then looked it over in the mirror.

I have to tell you, I was troubled. If you'll give me a little extra grace for some extreme girl-talk here, I'll explain. The suit had a "Wonder Woman" kind of thing happening. Remember Wonder Woman's *brass bra*? I never did understand what in the world that was all about. Especially since I tend to whine about mere underwire.

Anyway, evidently Wonder Woman and I do not have everything located in exactly the same place. I know, I know. I don't know why I was surprised either. I knew immediately the sturdy suit wasn't going to work. Brass or no brass, I don't want "them" around my waist. Too low or too high—it's really one of those Goldilocks kind of things. It has to be "just right." And when it's not, it's disturbing.

Searching for the Perfect Suit . . . And Its Contents

I tossed the wonder suit aside and picked up one that contained nothing whatsoever that was remotely brass related. Nothing. No cups. All spandex. It said on the tag that it was my size, but the entire suit was about the size of my thigh. Lycra is amazing stuff. No doubt that suit would've stretched from here to Malaysia. It took me a good ten minutes to writhe my way into the thing. But it went on! I thought that was a great victory until I turned around to look in the mirror . . . and—shock of all shocks—"they" were completely gone!

I looked high and low, over and under. I thought for a minute maybe I left them in the other suit. And in fact, I looked over at that Wonder Woman suit, and it really did look like they were still in there.

I was just about to panic. What do you do when you've looked everywhere and just can't find your bosom?

I think I finally found most of one of them under my left shoulder blade. How did it get back there? I found it almost by chance. I looked over my shoulder at the back of myself in the mirror. Talk about unsettling. I really couldn't tell if I was coming or going. I'm not sure which is more alarming: the fact that I found that first one so far out of its original orbit or the fact that I'm not sure I ever really found the other one.

I wondered how many gazillion hours of aerobic purse shopping it would take to shore up this kind of problem. Hey, these are not like ears. It's bad enough if they hang low, wobble to and fro. And even if I can tie 'em in a knot or tie 'em in a bow, I don't want to be able to throw them over my shoulder like a continental soldier.

Sadly, that was not the only problem area. I think cellulite must repel Lycra. Maybe that's why 97 percent of the cellulite squirms its way out of every opening. Have you ever had to watch your thighs ooze out the leg holes of a swimsuit? Even on a relatively small woman, oozing thighs are a disconcerting sight to be sure.

Two suits and I was finished trying on. It was clear by then that I hadn't made anywhere near enough coffee. And by the way, all the black suits were very appropriate because by the time I left there, I was in mourning. It's the kind of thing that can agitate a gal right past the mailbox and on to the treadmill.

Exercising Self-Control

Swim suit shopping is not the only thing that encourages exercise. On the spiritual side, the self-control that 1 Peter 1:13 refers to doesn't just happen. The New Living Translation says to "exercise self-control." I love that reminder to "exercise" it. We have to continually give over selfish thoughts, desires, ambitions, motives, and actions and exchange them for Spirit-controlled thoughts, desires, ambitions, motives, and actions. Those are the kind of reps that will build real spiritual muscle.

First Timothy 4:7–9 in *The Message* gives us the reminder to "Exercise daily in God—no spiritual flabbiness, please! Workouts in the gymnasium are useful, but a disciplined life in God is far more so, making you fit both today and forever. You can count on this. Take it to heart."

You really can take it to heart. Living a disciplined, self-controlled spiritual life is answering the call to obedience. It's surrendering to selfless, Christ-focused living. And every time we surrender, we're building holiness muscle. There's true fitness there, even if you never reach, stretch, or perk.

Self-control is the treadmill that leads to living that strong and disciplined life of holiness. We're doing spiritual crunches every time we exercise self-control in the areas of praying, studying God's Word, worshiping, reaching out to people who don't know Jesus, serving, and loving others.

Pursuing holiness is making sure we're working out in that self-control gym—and doing it with a lot more heart than I do in my physical exercise routine. Our spiritual goals should be set high and they should stay high (and we'll chat more specifically about setting those goals in chapter 19). We can depend on our faithful Father to accomplish every worthy goal, all glory to him!

As for the physical goals, I confess I'm aiming lower. As a matter of fact, it would be enough for me if I could end up with 10 percent or less of my body included in the ooze factor.

> If you instruct the brethren in these things, you will be a good minister of Jesus Christ, nourished in the words of faith and of the good doctrine which you have carefully followed. But reject profane and old wives' fables, and exercise yourself toward godliness. For bodily exercise profits a little, but godliness is profitable for all things, having promise of the life that now is and of that which is to come. This is a faithful saying and worthy of all acceptance. For to this end we both labor and suffer reproach, because we trust in the living God, who is the Savior of all men, especially of those who believe. These things command and teach.
>
> 1 Timothy 4:6–11 NKJV

---

3 Purpose in the Purse

Every time there's a formal event, I get to sift through my little collection of what I call my "dinky purse-ettes." Part of the novelty of the purse-ettes is that they're in such jarring contrast with my usual big-mama-mega-purse-o-rama. Big Mama holds my huge assortment of everyday necessities with room left over for a neck massager. That works out well, since carrying around the mega-bag frequently causes neck spasms.

Putting the two purses side by side is like putting a Great Dane next to a Chihuahua. There's something that's just plain fun about the weird dissimilarity. Big Mama could *eat* the dinky purse and it wouldn't even count as an appetizer.

It's a little problematic when I'm on the road for one of those formal occasions, though, since that dinky purse is for looks only. All those essential everyday necessities? They have to stay back in the hotel room. I don't have room in that little purse to even daydream about the neck massager. The dinky formal purse holds a hotel key. And that's about it. As a matter of fact, at the last event, I was afraid I might even have to *fold* that key card.

My husband asked what possible purpose there could be in carrying a cute mini-purse that won't hold anything. I tried to explain to him that in my mind, the emphasis in that phrase is on the word "cute." I'm willing to sacrifice the space for the cuteness.

A Purse in a Pill?

I confess, I do wonder how low they're going to go. How small will the purses get? I mean, if I can, in fact, carry several of the micro-bags inside my big mamma of a purse, I almost have to agree with my hubby: what's the purpose of that?

While we're enjoying "Supersize Me" everyday bags, designers seem to be able to take the formal purse somewhere near the protozoa zone. If they could only make the protozoa purse a little more usable—expandable, maybe.

It makes me think of those little capsules my kids used to get. Each one held some sort of surprise inside. They could put a Tylenol-sized capsule in the tub and in a few seconds, voilà! Ocean mammal! I'm wondering how much stuff I could fit into my purse if I dehydrated it all down to capsule size. Wouldn't it be great to just toss your favorite handbag contents into the sink and hydrate the whole thing into a fully stocked party purse? If everything I needed was capsule-sized, I could fit it all into the dinkiest of the party purses. And can't you just imagine looking inside your clutch and saying, "Oh look, I just remembered I brought a mariachi band. Could I have a glass of water?"

There are other belongings, large and small, that we can find in our purses that are even more surprising. Some even unsettling. Here are a few to ponder.

Top Ten Most Unsettling Things to Find in Your Purse

1. The ticket stub to a movie you don't remember seeing
2. The key to a gas station restroom you patronized somewhere in Idaho on your last vacation
3. Raisins (in a bag that looks just like the one you put your grapes in)
4. Chapstick that claims to be lip-flavored
5. A hand grenade
6. The pin of a hand grenade
7. Your weird Uncle Frank's toupee
8. Pepper spray in a spray bottle that looks just like Chanel No. 5
9. A bottle containing your weird Uncle Frank's kidney stone (that's when you decide you really should stop taking your purse with you when you visit weird Uncle Frank—or at least keep your Chanel No. 5 handy)
10. A mariachi band

Life Is Like a Bunch of Purses—You Never Know What You're Going to Get

Life is at least as full of surprises as the most unsettling purse. I have to confess, there have been unsettling times for me as I've sought to live holy. Those times, for instance, when I've been so determined to be a holy person—to live righteously. I've prayed in the morning, "O God, make me holy." Then so many times, by noon or so, the goal of holiness has long been crushed, and I find myself pray-whining something more like, "O God, can't you please just *force* me to live holy?" People talk about how God doesn't want to make us into robots. Maybe it's strange of me, but there are loads of times I would welcome being a robot for Christ if it meant I could consistently live in holiness. It can be so frustrating.

Paul dealt with it too. *The Message* phrases Paul's struggle this way in Romans 7:15–16: "What I don't understand about myself is that I decide one way, but then I act another, doing things I absolutely despise. So if I can't be trusted to figure out what is best for myself and then do it, it becomes obvious that God's command is necessary."

But self-control is in fact not so much about gritting my teeth and determining to do better. It's not robotically going through the legalistic motions. No, it's more of a surrender to his Spirit and a retraining of my thinking and my responses.

How do we retrain? God's Word. "Every Scripture is God-breathed (given by His inspiration) and profitable for instruction, for reproof and conviction of sin, for correction of error and discipline in obedience, [and] for training in righteousness (in holy living, in conformity to God's will in thought, purpose, and action)" (2 Timothy 3:16 AMP).

If we had a Bible in a capsule, we wouldn't even have to add water to see it blossom in the most glorious way into holy, purpose-filled living. "Training in righteousness . . . holy living"!

The Word on Holy Living

Every time we pick up his Word, it's like he's breathing into our lives everything we need to think as he thinks and everything we need to live in a way that honors and pleases him—everything we need for holy living. When we're consistently in God's Word, it becomes part of our thinking. It shows up in the way we behave and the way we respond. What a wonderful surprise it is to find ourselves conforming more to the image of Christ. Not an unsettling surprise, but a surprise that's better than the best mariachi band. It's the delightful surprise of sensing the Holy Spirit breathing his own sweet music of righteousness and purpose into our lives.

Without giving God's Word a prominent place in our lives—without making it a part of every day—we're not truly pursuing holiness. In Psalm 119:4–8, the psalmist offers a "holy pursuit" kind of prayer: "You have charged us to keep your commandments carefully. Oh, that my actions would consistently reflect your principles! Then I will not be disgraced when I compare my life with your commands. When I learn your righteous laws, I will thank you by living as I should! I will obey your principles" (NLT[a]).

Who's In Control?

"Self-control" in righteous living is not a shove-the-Spirit-aside-and-let-self-take-over kind of control. It's disciplining ourselves to allow the Spirit to control more and more. And it requires the discipline of filling our minds with his Word.

Maybe you haven't been building the discipline of reading God's Word into your life in a consistent way. If not, are you ready to commit to spending time with him in this holy pursuit? Ask him to give you the discipline, the self-control, to make his Word a regular part of your day and to see it as an enormously essential part of your day. It's a prayer he longs to answer.

As you're spending time in the Bible each day, pray through his message to you. Ask him to show you new truths and to help you apply them. Ask yourself if the passage reveals anything unholy in your life. Is there a sin you need to confess or are there any changes you need to make? Are there promises you're ready to claim? Are there good examples of holy living? Bad examples? Is there anything you need to learn about pursuing holiness? Anything that leads you into worshiping the Holy One? Anything the passage reminds you to thank him for?

It doesn't matter what size purse we carry—if we're toting the purse-protozoa or lugging Big Mama—keeping God's Word at our fingertips and staying faithfully connected, making it part of our thinking and part of our lives, is a powerful way to "be self-controlled." And that's exactly how we can grow more and more in living the holy life of purpose he's called us to live.

Incidentally, if you opt for the dehydrated purse contents, be careful not to mistake any of those capsules for your pain reliever. You think you had a headache before? Imagine the head waiter saying, "Excuse me, ma'am, your mariachi band is disturbing the other guests. Could you please turn the volume down on your abdomen?" That would take some Extra-Extra-Extra-Strength Tylenol—and an equal shot of Mylanta.

Our LORD, you bless everyone
who lives right
and obeys your Law.
You bless all of those
who follow your commands
from deep in their hearts
and who never do wrong
or turn from you.
You have ordered us always
to obey your teachings;

I don't ever want to stray
from your laws.
Thinking about your commands
will keep me from doing
some foolish thing.
I will do right and praise you
by learning to respect
your perfect laws.

Psalm 119:1–7 CEV

Hole in One? 4

I know man-bags are still on the unusual side, but I can hardly think of any guy who doesn't need a purse. A guy can carry a computer bag and his masculinity never comes into question. And I've never seen anyone wince at a man carrying a golf bag—that's even macho. But a handbag? The guys are just not there yet. They have to hang their cell phones on their clothes, for crying out loud. When a guy talks about a hole in one, there's no way he's talking about a purse with a leak. It's almost without exception a golf course thing.

Of course, even though most guys will claim adamantly that they don't do purses, they do have pockets that can be fairly purse-like, if you ask me. My 14-year-old son, Daniel, is a purse-pocket kind of guy. He was getting ready to do his laundry the other day. I was so happy when I looked over to see him emptying out the pockets of his jeans. All too often whatever is in the kids' pockets gets washed. We end up following the *thunk, thunk* noise until we find the pocket contents melted into one giant goo-ball in the dryer.

Nothing Up My Sleeve . . .

I went from "so happy" to "extremely fascinated" when I saw everything he was pulling out of those pockets. It was quite amazing really—his jeans were the hat, Daniel was the magician. He just kept pulling out more and more stuff.

He pulled out some Tootsie Roll wrappers. Then a few seconds later he pulled out about a half-dozen furry Tootsie Rolls. I think he had the entire year's worth of notes from his history class in one pocket, and I'm just sure I saw his trombone sheet music in the other. And speaking of hole in one, there were enough golf tees in his back pocket to get him through most of high school. How did he sit on those spiky things and not end up with any holes in his pocket?

He seemed pretty excited when he found the lunch money he'd been missing. But both of us were disturbed when we saw what looked like something from a science lab. A big hunk of something that we couldn't identify. And it looked like it was frying in its own juices. Gross. What was more disturbing was that he didn't throw it away.

I wondered how the kid could even sit down with all that stuff (the bubbling stuff and the non-bubbling stuff) in his jeans. All I could say was, "Daniel. Son. You need a purse."

It's funny that he's carrying around half his life in his jeans. It's even funnier that he has to keep pulling it all out every day when he changes clothes and then stuffing it all right back in the clean jeans. Anyone else wondering why a person would keep stuffing furry Tootsie Rolls and an unidentified frying object back into his pockets?

Time to Empty Those Pockets

It's even weirder when we let it become a habit to carry around spiritual junk we don't need, hanging on to stuff just because we've gotten used to it. Purse or no purse, if we're carrying around sinful stuff, it's past time to get rid of it.

Being self-controlled in getting rid of sin only happens as we submit to the first part of the passage, the part we looked at in the introduction: "prepare your minds for action." There's no self-control without action—or without "thinking clearly." And there's no clear thinking without self-control. It's amazing how preparing for action, thinking clearly, and being self-controlled work so closely together.

We need to stay on active alert and persevere in the area of self-control when it comes to any sin habits we continue to stuff back into our pockets. First Peter 5:8 charges us to do just that: "Be self-controlled and alert. Your enemy the devil prowls around like a roaring lion looking for someone to devour." The Enemy would love to see you sidetracked from the pursuit of holiness and rendered powerless by sneaky sin. As soon as we're aware of any speck of unholiness in our lives, we need to get rid of it, not wait for the Evil One to exploit it.

Anytime we catch a glimpse of sin in our lives, it's time to do the spiritual laundry—taking the junk out, then being washed clean by the blood of Jesus. (We'll look at getting rid of sin and getting clean in more detail in chapter 22.) There's nothing like having our whites whiter and our brights brighter!

Unbalanced Load

Sad to say, we sometimes find ourselves getting rid of those pesky sins at our holy laundry time, then the next day we stuff a handful of them right back in. Let's stay alert and be ever-ready to dump that sin right back out. Let's be self-controlled and not give up. That's the way to make sure we're not nonchalantly strolling behind holiness, or even jogging casually after it, but really and truly chasing it down, pursuing it with passionate zeal.

And it's amazing how beautifully freeing it is to stop lugging that junk around. Nothing frying or fermenting. Talk about feeling lighter! That's exactly how we're called to live. We're not merely encouraged to live holy. We're called to live holy. Look again at 1 Thessalonians 4:7, which says, "For God did not call us to be impure, but to live a holy life."

> O Lord, may we learn to rely on you more and more to produce a pure and holy life in us, according to your calling—a clean life of self-control that will magnify and glorify your name!

Can you imagine how many incredible and powerful things we'll see happen in our lives when we make that our heart's prayer every time we talk to the Father?

And speaking of seeing incredible things (all UFOs aside), I'm a little more wary now when I see Daniel cleaning out his pockets. I guess I should talk to him again about what he keeps shoving in there. First I want to throw away the handful of furry Tootsie Rolls I saw in my purse. I don't want to be hypocritical.

> As we know Jesus better, his divine power gives us everything we need for living a godly life. He has called us to receive his own glory and goodness! And by that same mighty power, he has given us all of his rich and wonderful promises. He has promised that you will

escape the decadence all around you caused by evil desires and that you will share in his divine nature.

So make every effort to apply the benefits of these promises to your life. Then your faith will produce a life of moral excellence. A life of moral excellence leads to knowing God better. Knowing God leads to self-control. Self-control leads to patient endurance, and patient endurance leads to godliness. Godliness leads to love for other Christians, and finally you will grow to have genuine love for everyone. The more you grow like this, the more you will become productive and useful in your knowledge of our Lord Jesus Christ.

2 Peter 1:3–8 NLT[a]

5 Polka-dot Purse

Have you ever had one of those little loaves of really great banana bread left over from a lunch out? Really great banana bread is not something you can just leave on the plate for the busboy to toss out like so much garbage—especially not an entire mini-loaf. No, if you're like the uncultured rest of us, you wrap that puppy up in a napkin and tuck it away in the large side pocket of your purse.

Then if you're less like the average rest of us and more like . . . well . . . me . . . you forget about it until you smell something odiously weird and start to see creepy little moldy dots coming through the outside of your purse. That's when you realize the banana bread is coming dangerously close to taking over. When the polka dots start growing fur, it's very likely too late.

A fur-a-dot purse? It's just not the same. Maybe I need to start carrying good old burp-and-seal plasticware in my purse. I guess I could just get a shoulder strap for a salad keeper and I'd be ready for just about anything.

It's clear you can't carry a loaf around in a purse for very long before the polka dots will catch up with you. It happened to the Israelites too. In their wilderness wanderings, they couldn't pack leftovers in their purses either. God provided food for the day. But if they tried to hang on to it, the next day it would be moldy and wormy—polka-dotted to the disgusting max.

Manna Mania

Have you ever wondered if the Israelites ever tried to get clever with their daily manna? It's amazing that God provided their food each day like clockwork. But I do remember reading that they got a little whiny about eating the same thing day in and day out. I can picture them moaning about their taste bud oppression. Maybe they would whine something like, "Oh, the hu-manna-ty!"

Never mind that the manna was sweet and tasty. Exodus 16:31 says "it tasted like honey wafers" (NLT[b]). Hey, that sounds like dessert to me. I've never known dessert and oppression to be coupled, have you?

I wonder every now and then if the people of Israel ever tried to get creative. Do you think they ever tried new recipes? Mannawiches, maybe?

What if they got even more clever and made it into a loaf, then added berries? Wouldn't that make it "Berry Manna-loaf"? I wonder if too much Berry Manna-loaf would cause them to sing mellow songs and consider "music and passion always the fashion." Perhaps they could've kept the theme and added different fruits to make other tasty treats. They could've even tried a version of my favorite banana bread. They could call it "Copacabana-banana-manna."

Creamy Filling?

They could've come up with all kinds of fillings. Or maybe they were just too busy whining to get creative. I would make fun of them for that, but I'm afraid there are too many times I ask God to provide and then take it for granted when he does. Or worse, I complain about the way he does it. Worse still is when I know what I'm supposed to do and don't do it, or know what I'm not supposed to do and do it anyway—that same Romans 7:15 Paul quandary we touched on in chapter 3. How embarrassing that I am still so quick to be full of myself instead of being full of him. Talk about the wrong kind of filling. It's the complete opposite of clear thinking and self-control.

I already confessed to spending mornings on my face begging God to make me holy, then blowing it before noon. So what happens when I'm pursuing holiness and I miserably fail?

I get back up.

Self-control and discipline are about staying away from sin, but they're also about never giving up in the holiness pursuit. The Enemy would like nothing better than to sidetrack us spiritually, convincing us there's nothing we can do except stay stuck in our sin and weakness in a powerless, fruitless, purposeless life. But Proverbs 24:16 says, "For though a righteous man falls seven times, he rises again, but the wicked are brought down by calamity." Pursuing holiness doesn't mean we'll never fall. It means we keep getting back up and get right back in hot pursuit.

How beautiful it is that no matter how big my failure, my pitiful weakness, or my whiny lack of faith, God's mercy is bigger. What amazing grace. He demonstrated that grace and mercy again and again with the whining Israelites. Psalm 78 tells us,

> They willfully put God to the test
>   by demanding the food they craved.
> They spoke against God, saying,
>   "Can God spread a table in the desert?" . . .
> Yet he gave a command to the skies above
>   and opened the doors of the heavens;
> he rained down manna for the people to eat,
>   he gave them the grain of heaven.
> Men ate the bread of angels;
>   he sent them all the food they could eat. . . .
> They ate till they had more than enough,
>   for he had given them what they craved. . . .
> In spite of all this, they kept on sinning;
>   in spite of his wonders, they did not believe. . . .
> Yet he was merciful;
>   he forgave their iniquities.
>
> (vv. 18–19, 23–25, 29, 32, 38)

Mercy in Every Size

His mercy still shows up in our every whiny inadequacy today. It shows up at the precise moment of our repentance of even the biggest, ugliest sins. Even after I've been shallow and full of self, he graciously shows me mercy. Psalm 65:3 says, "Though we are overwhelmed by our sins, you forgive them all" (NLT[b]).

No need to whine. He is in control. He provides everything we need, and his mercy will always be as big as we need it to be.

Blow off our sin as if it doesn't matter? We all know that's no way to live. Pursuing holiness means growing in how accurately we see sin. And the more we pursue holiness, the more we hate sin. That's why Romans 6:1–2 gives us a clear "certainly not" in answer to the question, "What shall we say [to all this]? Are we to remain in sin in order that God's grace (favor and mercy) may multiply and overflow? Certainly not! How can we who died to sin live in it any longer?" (AMP).

Pursue holiness. Relish mercy. Just as the Israelites were to depend on God for his day-by-day manna provision, we can depend on him for the day-by-day mercy we need.

As for the purses we may or may not need, I found an adorable polka-dot purse last week when I was out shopping. I'd love to buy it. But honestly, how can I justify the expense when I know I can make my own?

> If you, O Lord, kept a record of sins,
> O Lord, who could stand?
> But with you there is forgiveness;
> therefore you are feared.
> I wait for the Lord, my soul waits,
> and in his word I put my hope.
> My soul waits for the Lord
> more than watchmen wait for the morning,
> more than watchmen wait for the morning.
> O Israel, put your hope in the Lord,
> for with the Lord is unfailing love
> and with him is full redemption.
> He himself will redeem Israel
> from all their sins.
>
> Psalm 130:3–8

Part 2

"Set your hope fully on the grace to be given you when Jesus Christ is revealed"

6 A Purse Verse

Have you ever seen a fully loaded purse? I'm talking about a purse with all the options. Pockets and folds, zippers and snaps. Secret flaps and hidden agendas that make you feel that just carrying the purse around for a few days is surely going to organize your life completely from the purse out. More buttons, gadgets, and special features than the fanciest SUV. It's a beautiful thing to behold.

If you're a purse salesperson and you're looking for an easy-sale target for an overloaded, fully-optioned bag, paint a bull's-eye on me—I'm your chump. Okay, I might have to draw the line at the antilock brakes. On the other hand, if you can convince me I really need a handbag with dependable stopping power, I'm still not ruling out a sale. I might consider the purchase simply because it complements my "I brake for purse sales" bumper sticker.

It's so reassuring to have a purse that's ready for anything. Inspiring even. As a matter of fact, just the thought inspired this purse "overload ode"—and a vodie-oh-do.

Ode to the Purse with the Major Overload

I once had a purse
That was so fully loaded

Every zipper and pocket
Was utterly bloated

Whatever the need
My purse had the fix
Food, makeup or meds
Jewelry, fish food or bricks

I just loved that purse
Every big part and small part
But then someone took it
And turned it into a Wal-Mart

A super center with a handle—I could handle that! Now we're talking about a fully loaded purse. And just think, I could take my purse into its own automotive department when the time rolled around for its 10,000-mile checkup.

Fully Loaded Hope

As fun as a purse so fully loaded would be, it's even more fun to think about the hope we have that is fuller still. I love this section of the 1 Peter 1 passage: "Set your hope fully on the grace to be given you when Jesus Christ is revealed."

We can set our hope fully on his grace. It's a full grace. That makes for a full hope. His grace is loaded to the max with every provision we'll ever need.

It reminds me in a tiny way of the big yellow chair we have in our family room. I love that thing. It's perfect for curling up with the laptop or a good book, watching a movie—whatever. Soft and cushy all over, curved and padded armrests. This chair's got everything.

The only downside of the big yellow chair is that everything that falls out of pockets and purses gets eaten by all the cush. It's like having our own personal Bermuda Triangle on the easterly side of the family room. Things just disappear in there.

If you could turn the yellow chair upside down and give it a good shake, you would no doubt think you'd hit the jackpot. The last time we gave it a shake (and it took three of us to do it), it rained enough change for a couple of cheeseburgers, fries, and a chocolate shake or two—all super-sized.

That chair really does have everything. Besides the money, out tumbled my good lip gloss, a bite-sized Snickers, my checkbook (I'd been looking for that thing), hand lotion, two ink pens, and nail polish in three different shades. That's when I realized I had the same kinds of provisions in my yellow chair that I have in my purse. Maybe more. Come to think of it, the yellow chair is often about as fully loaded as one of those "Wal-Mart in a handbag" kinds of purses!

There were mints in there too. I would never want to actually put one of them in my mouth, mind you. It would take too long to pick that much fuzz off a Tic Tac. I will point out, however, that mints that come with the fiber built right in would likely promote better colon health *and* fresher breath. One more need met! All in all, if that yellow chair had a shoulder strap, I could conceivably haul it along as a handbag without missing anything I need.

Better Than the Best Chair/Purse

I love to think about how our heavenly Father provides for us in the biggest "Wal-Mart–purse/yellow-chair" kind of way. Our God provided our salvation—our one true eternal need. It's the provision that sealed and settled our eternity in heaven with him. And within that salvation is everything else we need, to boot. If our salvation were the yellow chair, all the goodies inside would be his faithful provision for our every daily need. Paul reminds us in Philippians 4:19, "And my God will meet all your needs according to his glorious riches in Christ Jesus."

Is there anything we truly need that he doesn't provide? No! He provides for us here and now, and he provides for our marvelous future in heavenly ways we can hardly begin to imagine. Revelation 21 gives us a little glimpse:

> I saw the Holy City, the new Jerusalem, coming down out of heaven from God, prepared as a bride beautifully dressed for her husband. And I heard a loud voice from the throne saying, "Now the dwelling of God is with men, and he will live with them. They will be his people, and God himself will be with them and be their God. He will wipe every tear from their eyes. There will be no more death or mourning or crying or pain, for the old order of things has passed away." . . . It shone with the glory of God, and its brilliance was like that of a very precious jewel, like a jasper, clear as crystal. . . . The wall was made of jasper, and the city of pure gold, as pure as glass. The foundations of the city walls were decorated with every kind of precious stone. The first foundation was jasper, the second sapphire, the third chalcedony, the fourth emerald, the fifth sardonyx, the sixth carnelian, the seventh chrysolite, the eighth beryl, the ninth topaz, the tenth chrysoprase, the eleventh jacinth, and the twelfth amethyst. The twelve gates were twelve pearls, each gate made of a single pearl. The great street of the city was of pure gold, like transparent glass. I did not see a temple in the city, because the Lord God Almighty and the Lamb are its temple. The city does not need the sun or the moon to shine on it, for the glory of God gives it light, and the Lamb is its lamp. . . . Nothing impure will ever enter it, nor will anyone who does what is shameful or deceitful, but only those whose names are written in the Lamb's book of life.
>
> Revelation 21:2–4, 11, 18–23, 27

So much finer than the biggest Wal-Mart or the cushiest chair of yellow. Walls of jasper and shining streets of gold. What an amazing place! But do you know what will make it heaven? It's the presence of Jesus. God the Father and Jesus the Son will even light the place! We will be able to live with our Savior, walking with him and talking with him. It doesn't get finer than that.

Dwelling on God's glorious provision makes me feel so very rich. We're richer than the richest. We're richer than any gal who owns her own Wal-mart in a bag. It's a richness in his grace that gives us hope. Partial hope? Partial grace? Oh no. To the fullest.

In every way that truly counts, we're fully loaded!

> To those who have received (obtained an equal privilege of) like precious faith with ourselves in and through the righteousness of our God and Savior Jesus Christ: May grace (God's favor) and peace (which is perfect well-being, all necessary good, all spiritual prosperity, and freedom from fears and agitating passions and moral conflicts) be multiplied to you in [the full, personal, precise, and correct] knowledge of God and of Jesus our Lord. For His divine power has bestowed upon us all things that [are requisite and suited] to life and godliness, through the [full, personal] knowledge of Him Who called us by and to His own glory and excellence (virtue). By means of these He has bestowed on us His precious and exceedingly great promises, so that through them you may escape [by flight] from the moral decay (rottenness and corruption) that is in the world because of covetousness (lust and greed), and become sharers (partakers) of the divine nature. . . .
>
> Because of this, brethren, be all the more solicitous and eager to make sure (to ratify, to strengthen, to make steadfast) your calling and election; for if you do this, you will never stumble or fall.
>
> Thus there will be richly and abundantly provided for you entry into the eternal kingdom of our Lord and Savior Jesus Christ.
>
> 2 Peter 1:1–4, 10–11 AMP

7 There's a Face in My Handbag

I was digging through my purse recently when I noticed that about 90 percent of the contents were cosmetics related. That bothered me a little. I wondered if I was lugging around a bit too much vanity. And how much of that stuff did I even use? I had products in there to take the color out of my face and more products to put the color back in. Lotions, colors, creams, and serums—it looked like I had enough potions in there to build a separate face, weird though it would be. Of course, if I made my own monster-face, mine would have even skin tone and some really great lashes.

Here's Lookin' at You, Kid

Eyes, cheeks, brows, lips—when I put it all together, there was an entire face in there! Maybe you can imagine how alarming it is to look into your purse and realize it's looking back at you.

I guess it's good that when I'm trying to put my best face forward, as it were, I have at least a couple of them to choose from. If you ask me, being two-faced is not always such a bad thing. Those of you who are over forty have likely already figured out that any face nearing that half-century mile marker requires a lot more equipment. Just keeping it from pooling at my chest is a challenge these days. I guess eventually I'll have to find a purse that will hold some major hydraulics. Do they make a high-powered jack in a purse-sized model?

Other unusual makeup items you might find in a purse? How about these?

Top Ten Makeup-Related Items You Rarely Find in a Normal Person's Purse

1. Do-it-yourself Botox Kit (there may soon come a day)
2. The specially illuminated Easy-Tweezy 3000 with its patented electrolysis attachment
3. A sandblaster (it's the frugal girl's dermabrasion kit)
4. The "Get Fit Like Arnold" Gym-in-a-Bag
5. A vat of Polynesian facial mud
6. Inflatable cheekbones
7. Jamaican lash extensions
8. The last 14 issues of *Cover-Cosmo-Style-Vogue-Fashion-Plate Girl Magazine*
9. A fold-out massage table
10. A masseuse to go with the massage table

I may not have the Easy-Tweezy (though I really am very interested) or any of those other items in my purse, "purse-say," but I will admit that it takes a lot of equipment to pull off the makeup routine these days. It's a lot of stuff to lug.

When it comes to our spiritual lives, there are much more fruitful things to lug. Too often we spend all our spiritual energy carrying all the wrong baggage. We "hope" we can get our lives back in order. That kind of "hope-so hope" is no hope at all. Where does 1 Peter 1:13 tell us to set our hope? On the grace of Jesus! "Set your hope fully on the grace to be given you when Jesus Christ is revealed."

And an amazing grace it is. I quickly and freely admit that the author of this great hymn wrote a much more poignant verse than my purse verse from the last chapter:

> Amazing grace, how sweet the sound
> That saved a wretch like me.
> I once was lost but now I'm found,
> Was blind but now I see. . . .
>
> When we've been there ten thousand years
> Bright shining as the sun,
> We've no less days to sing God's praise
> Than when we first begun.[1]

Our focus verse in 1 Peter speaks of the grace of Jesus that will be revealed when he comes again. It will be the magnificent culmination of his grace-plan. His plan of grace was put into motion in the Garden of Eden when Adam and Eve sinned. His plan of grace was centered at the coming of his Son, Jesus, to pay for their sin and ours. "For the grace of God that brings salvation has appeared to all men" (Titus 2:11). The next verse further tells us how that affects our pursuit of holiness in the here and now: "It teaches us to say 'No' to ungodliness and worldly passions, and to live self-controlled, upright and godly lives in this present age" (v. 12). Even more about our future grace: "while we wait for the blessed hope—the glorious appearing of our great God and Savior, Jesus Christ, who gave himself for us to redeem us from all wickedness and to purify for himself a people that are his very own, eager to do what is good" (vv. 13–14).

Past, present, and future—his amazing grace is there for us anyplace, anytime, and for anything.

And I Do Mean Anything

Those times when we begin to lug around the ugly effects of guilt, it's good to remember that grace. The guilt? Okay, we've earned it. We were born with it (I'm so tempted in this make-up-themed chapter to add "Maybe we're born with it; maybe it's Maybelline"). Since sin entered the world in that garden rebellion, we've all inherited a sin nature. And we are guilty.

But the glorious truth is that Jesus paid our guilt penalty when he "gave himself for us to redeem us from all wickedness" as verse 14 reminded us. Do we still need to lug the guilt? If we've confessed and forsaken the sin that brought it on, no! God's grace is the most magnificent guilt-eraser.

I've been blessed to meet such wonderful women from one side of this nation to the other. But I so hurt for my girlfriends—so many of them—who are stifled, stumped, and stuck in guilt.

If you're one of my "stuck" girlfriends, spend some time thinking about his amazing grace, will you? Don't waste his grace. Bask in it. Let it cause you to love him and worship him in a new and powerful way. Let it inspire you to pursue holiness like never before. Let it remind you that you don't have to live stuck in the guilt of past failures. You don't have to carry the big, ugly bag of guilt. That's one accessory we just don't need.

If it's been awhile since you celebrated his amazing grace, sing a few verses in your heart. Get free. You don't need to live your life in a wince, constantly waiting for the heavenly Father to lower the boom on you for the sin that's already been forgiven through Christ. Stop lugging guilt that's no longer yours! Don't stuff it in a purse, pulling it out again and again to see how ugly it is, memorizing each offense, remembering every ugly detail. His amazing grace has already dealt with every wretched thing you've confessed. It's gone!

On top of it all, we so often convince ourselves that there's a hidden sin we don't know about that we haven't confessed. Guilt upon guilt. If you're experiencing guilt over a real sin issue in your life, let it inspire you to deal with it, confessing and forsaking it. Trust your heavenly Father to reveal to you anything he wants you to get rid of. He is big enough and loving enough to do that. But don't waste time wrestling with a sneaky shadow of guilt or guilt that the blood of Jesus covered long ago.

The Guilt Game

Did you know that one of the Enemy's most successful games is the guilt game? I think our guilt is likely one of his favorite toys. When we're weighted down with it, we're beaten down before we even get into the spiritual battle. There's no power to live a holy life if we are stuck in the shame and defeat of guilt.

But isn't staying trapped in the never-ending guilt game like saying, "Yes, Jesus' death was enough for the sin and failures of others, but it surely couldn't be enough for mine"? Silly thinking, isn't it? Don't play the Enemy's game.

God's amazing grace and forgiveness is as real and complete as his death on the cross and his magnificent resurrection three days later. If you're struggling with guilt over a sin you've already confessed to the Lord, you're letting all the power for pursuing holiness drain right out of your life. Understand with new conviction that his death was enough. Embrace the sweet freedom there is in his complete forgiveness.

The Lord wants to free you from guilt by his amazing grace: "In Christ we are set free by the blood of his death. And so we have forgiveness of sins. How rich is God's grace" (Ephesians 1:7 NCV). Live with a heart so full of his rich grace and so focused on that forgiving grace that the guilt you've been hauling around will stomp off pouting, upset that it's no longer your focus.

You're going to love the free life. As a matter of fact, I can picture you beginning the next step in your pursuit of holiness by pulling out the fold-out massage table and your purse masseuse for a celebratory spa day.

> But because of his great love for us, God, who is rich in mercy, made us alive with Christ even when we were dead in transgressions—it is by grace you have been saved. And God raised us up with Christ and seated us with him in the heavenly realms in Christ Jesus, in order that in the coming ages he might show the incomparable riches of his grace, expressed in his kindness to us in Christ Jesus. For it is by grace you have been saved, through faith—and this not from yourselves, it is the gift of God.
>
> Ephesians 2:4–8

8

Oh Purse Feathers!

My good friend Peanuts Rudolph has given me a lot of purse counsel over the years. Mind you, I don't listen to all of her handbag advice since one of her purses, for instance, has extremely long, extremely hot pink fur. The longest of fur in the hottest of pink. And anytime a purse requires more hair products than I do, I'm simply not willing to invest in it.

But there are a couple of pieces of purse advice she's offered that I've taken to heart far and above the rest. First, she said that a woman should never carry a purse bigger than her rear end. For some reason, that makes sense to me. Unfortunately, most of the time that still leaves me with a "wide" variety of choices. Peanuts also warns that your handbag should never be smaller than the total area of one bun. I valued that piece of purse counsel too.

I have those two main rules down, but I still have measurement questions. I've wondered, for instance, how her fur purse measures up in the purse-choice process. Would she measure from side to side, strap to liner, or start at the end of the fur and work her way up? The same question "rears" its head when there's fringe. And how do feathers figure in? You'll have to trust me that Peanuts, wild purse woman that she is, will have to consider this feather-measuring question somewhere along the line in her purse life journey. So do the feathers count in the main circumference sum when you're calculating the rear-to-purse ratio? These are important numbers to consider, especially when you're getting ready for a big event.

Ready or Not

I was getting ready for a special event a few months ago. We were shooting a video designed to tell a little about the book *High Heels in High Places*. One of the most exciting aspects of the video shoot was that we did the filming in, of all great places, a shoe store. I was surrounded by shoes and purses! Accessory heaven—and I think I could still count it all as book research.

I knew I needed to choose just the right accessories—and just the right outfit. Two days before we were scheduled to shoot, I told my husband that it was time to get ready, and I started rifling through suits, skirts, shoes, and purses for just the right combo. I remember saying to Richie something like, "Okay, now that it's time to get ready, I need to lose twenty pounds in two days. Think that's going to be a problem?"

Guess what. It was. After all, you can definitely call it a problem, can't you, when the skirt you're planning to wear will only fit on one thigh at a time? It was obvious I was going to be hunting around at the last minute for a much bigger purse. Much bigger. Or maybe gluing on a lot of extra purse feathers.

A disciplined person would've started the weight-loss project a few months before. And actually, I did. It's just that someone sent over a huge, exceptionally gorgeous chocolate cake. That's when I decided that the weight-loss plans were "to be continued." After the chocolate cake came a buffet with my name on it. Then there was that cheesecake. Before I knew it, there was no time left for doing my "continuing." Last-minute readying doesn't work when there's a twenty-pound surplus of "to be continueds."

Continuing the Continuing

I hope I never catch myself "readying" in the same way for Jesus' coming. "When Jesus Christ is revealed"—oh what a day that will be! Do you know what 1 John 2:28 instructs me to do? Continue! "And now, dear children, continue in him, so that when he appears we may be confident and unashamed before him at his coming." These are not instructions to continue in trying to lose weight or find the right purse—they're not really even instructions to try to live right. They are instructions to continue "in him." The verse right before this one says that we are to "remain in him."

Thinking about Jesus' return can be such a great encouragement to remain in tight and continuing fellowship with him. It has a purifying effect on our lives. Obeying him, communicating with him in prayer, reading his Word, serving him, loving him wholeheartedly—that's how we "continue in him." That's the way to pursue holiness and to live a fulfilling life. All cheesecake issues aside, it's a life that we don't have to be embarrassed about when we hear the trumpet.

And being ready for his return is eternally more important than anything else we'll ever get ready for. Isn't it incredible how enthusiastically we can get ready for certain things? There are times when I get a phone call that a friend is on her way over, and before I hang up the phone, I'm in hyper-cleaning mode. It's at times like these that I'm miraculously inspired to clean up the house at world-record-breaking pace, dishes flying into the dishwasher, shoes swiftly making their way to the closets. Some of you are pretending you don't know what I'm talking about here when you really do. But I'm telling you, with the right panic-driven inspiration, I can ready an embarrassingly messy family room in five minutes flat. It's impressive what I can do when I know someone is coming.

Guess Who's Coming Over

The most important someone of all time is coming. And I want to be ready. Not that "try to lose twenty pounds two days before" kind of ready. Not the last-minute rushing around stuffing shoes in closets kind of ready. No, I want to be waiting eagerly, expectantly, longingly, lovingly. I want to have my "house" already clean. I want him to find me pursuing holiness every day I'm waiting.

O Lord, let us live holy lives as we excitedly watch for your return.

Let's watch for him in a wholehearted, holy way!

And by the way, if you're ever watching videos and you run across the *High Heels* one, you may notice I'm wearing a hot pink jacket—no fur, no feathers. I'm also wearing a completely different skirt than originally planned. And the purse didn't make the cut at all. Feathers or no feathers, it never did measure up.

> Brothers, we do not want you to be ignorant about those who fall asleep, or to grieve like the rest of men, who have no hope. We believe that Jesus died and rose again and so we believe that God will bring with Jesus those who have fallen asleep in him. According to the Lord's own word, we tell you that we who are still alive, who are left till the coming of the Lord, will certainly not precede those who have fallen asleep. For the Lord himself will come down from heaven, with a loud command, with the voice of the archangel and with the trumpet call of God, and the dead in Christ will rise first. After that, we who are still alive and are left will be caught up together with them in the clouds to meet the Lord in the air. And so we will be with the Lord forever. Therefore encourage each other with these words. . . .
>
> May God himself, the God of peace, sanctify you through and through. May your whole spirit, soul and body be kept blameless at the coming of our Lord Jesus Christ.
>
> 1 Thessalonians 4:13–18; 5:23

9 I'm Packin' Heat—There's a Blow-dryer in Here

I was out shopping, and I caught sight of the most adorable pink suede purse. I instinctively reached for it, but then hesitated over some second thoughts. Should I go with the suede leather when it's so obviously weather/water-vulnerable? I pictured myself having to shove it under my skirt for cover in a surprise rain shower. A suede leather purse is nothing like a good letter carrier. Rain, sleet, snow—any one of those spot-generating precipitation disasters can halt whatever is on the to-do list of the suede-packing person. I think it's safe to say we'll never see a postal worker carrying the mail in a pink suede leather mailbag.

The suede vulnerability seems very strange to me since, even though a cow is probably covered with 99 percent leather (pink or not), I've never seen one ducking for cover in a storm. Can you picture a herd dashing for the barn in a rainstorm, mooing, "Hurry! Think what'll happen to all this leather!"

I Am Purse-sueded

I wonder why we make such a fuss over what a purse is made of anyway. Animal rights issues aside and tongue placed firmly in cheek, while cow is acceptable and alligator can be fancy, where are all the possum purses? Armadillo would make a sturdy purse, wouldn't it? Why does it matter which animal? I've seen faux leopard and zebra, but I've never seen anything peddled as faux donkey. Goat? None. Fox but no cat, mink but no rat. There seem to be a few inconsistencies.

It's obvious why we never run across porcupine, but I wonder if a kangaroo purse would have extra pockets. Who couldn't love a designer original of a fake marsupial?

And while we're on the topic, if you know you're going to be out in the rain, why not a duckskin purse? I'm telling you, that kind of purse could be a fair-weather friend *and* a foul-weather friend too (or "fowl" weather friend?). And haven't we already decided that a few feathers can be a nice touch anyway?

If you're ducking the duck and sticking with the suede, maybe it's a good idea to buy a little purse-shaped raincoat. (Maybe you're ducking the duck purse because you didn't like the "bill"—honest, I tried to resist adding that one, but just couldn't stop myself.) If not a purse raincoat, you might at least consider carrying a blow-dryer for any moisture emergencies. What could be more reassuring when you're toting leather accessories than the sound of a blow-dryer revving up its little engine?

We'll Understand It Better By and By

I admit it. There is so much I don't understand about pink purses and possum pelts. And so much I don't understand about much bigger issues as well.

First Corinthians 13:9–12 backs me up:

> For we know in part and we prophesy in part, but when perfection comes, the imperfect disappears. When I was a child, I talked like a child, I thought like a child, I reasoned like a child. When I became a man, I put childish ways behind me. Now we see but a

poor reflection as in a mirror; then we shall see face to face. Now I know in part; then I shall know fully, even as I am fully known."

I don't know it all. But someday I will. What hope that gives!

No need to wait until we completely understand it all to set our hope fully on his grace. When Jesus Christ is revealed, oh grace upon grace, we'll understand it all. We'll know the Lord as fully as he knows us, we're told. And he knows us inside out and upside down, through and through, from our deepest soul to the farthest end of our purse fringe. Our relationship will be transformed into one that is face to face, hand in hand. We will know him as he knows us.

Knowing that, and having our hope fully resting in that knowledge, makes enduring the "partial knowledge" of the here and now so much easier. Our "knowing" is coming. When Jesus comes, we will see clearly. We'll understand and experience holiness in a new and glorious way.

And when Jesus comes, he will fix everything that's hurt and broken.

Band-Aid Theology

I remember when my kids were small and a Band-Aid could fix just about anything. I had a house full of preschoolers so there were plenty of skinned knees and elbows. But I must say, there was never a boo-boo so great that one of those strips of padded plastic couldn't fix it. If the Band-Aid happened to have Barney or Superman on it, the healing powers increased about sevenfold. Miraculous!

It was amazing to me, too, that as soon as I bought a box of the coolest bandages, some kind of injury surfaced. What timing

I had! Interestingly, some of the injuries were not visible to the human eye. I often wondered how an invisible boo-boo could require six Band-Aids, but mine is not to reason why. Mine is just to peel the paper and affix Barney where it hurts. Nope, I don't understand it. But I just don't have to. It works.

How wonderful that the Lord's understanding is infinitely bigger than mine. Psalm 147:5 says, "Great is our Lord and mighty in power; his understanding has no limit." I don't have to understand the details of life. I don't have to have pink suede figured out, and there's no need for me to know how and why a Band-Aid miraculously heals. It's enough to understand that whatever the situation—whether I'm facing the visible or invisible impossible challenges of this life—in his understanding, he knows exactly what I need. There's no limit to what he knows, no limit to his mighty power, no "impossible" challenge for him. He has everything needed to meet every need.

So I really don't have to fret about the things I don't understand. I don't even have to fret about the aches and pains of living in this temporary body. Verse 3 of Psalm 147 says, "He heals the brokenhearted and binds up their wounds." You have to love that! Praise God for holy Band-Aids of the almighty kind!

Remembering how thoroughly he knows me inspires and revs me up for every holy pursuit like the most powerful blow-dryer. He knows the real me. And he loves me still. That makes me desire all the more to live for him in holiness. *Thank you, Father, that you are all-knowing and still ever-gracious and ever-loving!*

I don't need a pink suede faux possum skin Band-Aid. I'll be fine as long as my hope is fixed. And that hope is sure because his grace and love is oh so full. Nothing can separate me from that love. "For I am persuaded that neither death nor life, nor angels nor principalities nor powers, nor things present nor things to come, nor height nor depth, nor any other created thing, shall be able to separate us from the love of God which is in Christ Jesus our Lord" (Rom. 8:38–39 NKJV).

The Romans 8:38 kind of "persuaded" isn't about purses or suede. It means "I am convinced." That is a sure hope—a hope set "fully on the grace to be given you when Jesus Christ is revealed."

That's all the knowing I really need for now. Though if I decide to go with the purse raincoat for the suede leather, I may still need to know where to get some galoshes for the matching heels I found. Maybe something in faux armadillo?

> O LORD, You have searched me and know me.
> You know my sitting down and my rising up;
> You understand my thought afar off.
> You comprehend my path and my lying down,
> And are acquainted with all my ways.
> For there is not a word on my tongue,
> But behold, O LORD, You know it altogether.
> You have hedged me behind and before,
> And laid Your hand upon me.
> Such knowledge is too wonderful for me;
> It is high, I cannot attain it. . . .
> Search me, O God, and know my heart;
> Try me, and know my anxieties;
> And see if there is any wicked way in me,
> And lead me in the way everlasting.
>
> Psalm 139:1-6, 23-24 NKJV

10 Nurse the Purse

Whenever I travel, my purse takes on a whole new feel. It becomes more like an extra piece of luggage. Every vital item that doesn't fit into the suitcase gets tossed into the purse. I'll never forget the time I was trudging my way through the airport when tragedy struck. My purse strap snapped! And I still had security and about two dozen gates to go. Before making it to that last gate, I was in a sprint, in a lather, and the purse was dragging a couple of feet behind me. The strap had become sort of a leash for my pet purse.

I'm embarrassed to say that my untrained pet purse was flying so recklessly behind me that it ended up taking out a couple of businessmen, a cute hippie-looking lady, and an airline attendant pushing a wheelchair. I thought someone on the airport staff was going to make me kennel it before I could get to my gate. Heel, girl!

They have just about everything a traveler would ever need at the airport. But I was on the lookout through twenty-some-odd gates for a sign that read "This Way to the Purse First-Aid Station" and never found anything even similar. How far does a person have to lug a broken handbag before finding a purse nurse?

Purse 911

I don't think I'm the only one who needs a little purse CPR every now and then. I saw one lady whose pager had disappeared in her purse. It had somehow found a sneaky weak spot in the seam and gotten trapped inside the purse lining. I don't have to tell you that most airport security people are not long in the sense of humor department these days. Who can blame them? But it's that much more evident when you're stuck in security with a beeping purse lining. We've all seen enough action/adventure movies to know that a beeping purse can hardly be dismissed. I knew that the lady, poor thing, would be spending the day getting to know the security people really well if that beeper didn't come out of hiding.

Though I've never been known to travel light when it comes to the trip purse, I do try to remember to carry a purse that does not have a history of having a beeper-eating lining. I try to remember to at least take out a few things that I'm not going to need. For instance, why do I think I need to take that tire gauge in my purse when I'm on the road with no car? How about the shoe shine kit with the special battery-operated buffing accessory when I've only packed sandals? Sometimes I'm in and out of that purse so much it's like having a baby Grand Central Station.

Purse Central Station

Remembering to leave a few of those unnecessary extras behind can be a good thing. Beyond Purse Central Station, in the pursuit of holiness, we need to remember to let go of a few of those things in life we don't need. Sometimes our holiness pursuit is either encouraged or thwarted simply by what we choose to remember and what we choose to forget.

Paul said in Philippians 3:13–14, "Forgetting what is behind and straining toward what is ahead, I press on toward the goal to win the prize for which God has called me heavenward in Christ Jesus."

I wish I didn't have to admit to how many times I remember what I'm supposed to forget, hanging on to offenses and nursing grudges (and grudge-nursing is definitely not a healthy kind of first aid). It's like stuffing my purse full of everything I don't need and heading to the airport, shoulder strap flapping in the wind. In the same way, I then forget what I'm supposed to remember. Things like forgiving as I've been forgiven, loving unconditionally, and keeping a tight rein on those influences that tempt me to stumble. Those are not my holiest moments, to say the least.

Remembering to Forget

Forgetting what lies behind can be so freeing for us as we seek to live holy lives. Have you been hurt by someone? We live in a fallen world full of imperfect people. Hurt is inevitable. But hanging on to hurt, letting it sour into bitterness, will inhibit the pursuit of holiness every time.

Forgetting what lies behind can mean forgiving an offense, choosing not to hang on to it any longer. It can mean forgetting about our own failures, accepting God's gracious forgiveness, and moving forward. It can even be about forgetting the good things we've done. Sometimes those will stir up pride that will trip us up faster than a purse on a leash. We find ourselves taking credit for the things the Lord has accomplished through us instead of giving all glory to him.

When God's Word says, "Set your hope fully on the grace to be given you when Jesus Christ is revealed," that should be a reminder to us that the grace given to us is a grace we're supposed to extend to others too. The verse is also interpreted: "Look forward to the special blessings that will come to you at the return of Jesus Christ" (NLT[a]). Forgetting what lies behind, and "looking forward"!

Our Father is so good at forgetting and remembering—and knowing when to do which one. He says in Jeremiah 31:34, "For I will forgive their wickedness and will remember their sins no more." Do our sins simply slip his mind? Not the mind of an omniscient God. But it means he chooses to count them as ineffective, no longer holding them against us.

As for God's remembering, he's the best. The record is clear. All through the Bible God's promises are always kept as he remembers his people. Psalm 105:8 says, "He remembers his covenant forever." And God remembers with action. There is always "doing" behind his promises.

Likewise, when he forgets our sins, he is essentially *not* acting, not taking an action he's free to take in his omnipotence and holiness. Maybe you've been harboring unforgiveness and letting bitterness grow toward someone in your life because you figure if you can't forget it you haven't forgiven it. But "forgive and forget" doesn't mean you suddenly get a holy amnesia about a wound someone has caused. It means you're choosing to deny that bitter action. It means you're giving it to the Lord, not allowing that hurt to control you or let the memory haunt you.

When Paul was forgetting what was behind him, I think he was in essence refusing to allow anything from his past to hinder his love for Christ or his pursuit of holiness. Not embracing amnesia, but letting go of pain, pride, hate, or a desire for revenge.

Get Ready to Get Free

Let me encourage you, friend, to get rid of any bitterness that's deterring you in your pursuit of holiness. Unforgiveness is a prison. Let your heavenly Father set you free. That's just what he wants to do.

The emphasis is on *the Father*—letting him free you. Don't try to free yourself. You'll be stuck in that bitterness jail forever with no hope of parole. He has told you to forgive, so it's clearly his will. And he empowers you to do everything he wills you to do. It's his desire to see you free of all those encumbrances and fruitfully pursuing a holy life.

Have you been lugging around bitterness, rehashing the offense, dragging it behind you, letting it weigh you down? It's time to reel in the purse and get rid of the shoe shine kit, so to speak. Get rid of that bitterness you just don't need.

Remember that we started our pursuit in the beginning pages of this book with preparing our minds for action. That's how we pursue holiness. And once again, girlfriends, it's action time!

Need some help in the reeling and ridding? You can pray something like this:

> O Father, I've been hauling this bitterness for far too long. Lord, may today be the day I put that forgiveness into action—all by your power. Give me the strength to stop lugging that old grievance around, to stop pulling it out and rehashing it, to make forgiveness active. Each time I see the bitterness following me again, Lord, I pray that you will convict me instantly by your Holy Spirit to let it go. Oh Lord, let today be the day that I look forward. No turning back. Take me to a new holy place with you. Thank you, thank you, thank you for the freedom available to me through your Son. Help me to offer it freely to others. Through your power and because of Jesus, Amen.

There is freedom waiting for you at the end of that prayer. It's a prayer of holy action!

Incidentally, in other not-so-important purse matters, I had to take a different kind of action with the purse on a leash. After the airport ordeal, the poor little purse had to be put to sleep.

> Therefore, as God's chosen people, holy and dearly loved, clothe yourselves with compassion, kindness, humility, gentleness and patience. Bear with each other and forgive whatever grievances you may have against one another. Forgive as the Lord forgave you. And over all these virtues put on love, which binds them all together in perfect unity. Let the peace of Christ rule in your hearts, since as members of one body you were called to peace. And be thankful.
>
> Colossians 3:12–15

Part 3

“As obedient children”

11 Im-purse-onator

Full price for a designer purse or significantly less for a knock-off? Whose name is really on the bag? Big questions in purse-purchasing ethics! The real bummer is when you've spent the bucks on your designer original and get it home to find that your Prada is actually more of a Yada Yada. Instead of a Prada, you gotta lotta nada. It's purse-ona non grata.

Let's face it; the name can be oh so important.

No Other Name

I said I'd never do it, but here I am—the worst of them all. I said I'd never be one of those moms who went through the entire list of her kids' names before hitting on the right one. I think it makes each of the kids feel a little like a knockoff.

At least once a week when I'm wanting to say something to one of my kids (something of vital importance, I'm sure), it's suddenly a roll call. I hit every name on my five-kid list and sometimes even a cousin or two. Then to add even more offense, I somehow manage to get a couple of the pets mixed in. It's getting downright embarrassing. If I added a "Banana-fanna-fo," do you think they'd be fooled into thinking it was some kind of name game?

I could give up and number my kids, but I have no doubt I'd just call them the wrong numbers. "Five . . . no, I mean, Thr . . . doh . . . Four . . ." By the time you call your kids a few wrong numbers, they're likely to be insulted enough to tune you out anyway. *You have reached a kid that has been disconnected or is no longer listening.* Either that or they'll have a really good laugh at your expense.

What Did You Call Me?

I was chatting with a friend of mine the other day. I can't even remember why now, but somewhere in the conversation I had the perfect occasion to exclaim, "Surely you're kidding!" She said right back, "I'm totally not kidding! And don't call me Susan." Then we both pondered that in silence for a few seconds until she said, "Oh wait . . . it's *Shirley*, isn't it?"

And then I had a really good laugh at her expense.

Sometimes there's just no substituting the right name. In Acts 4, Peter and John were standing before the rulers trying to explain whose name they were using to do all the preaching and healing they had been doing—the preaching and healing they had just spent the night in jail for, by the way. Peter didn't need a roll call. He told them flat out, "Salvation is found in no one else, for there is no other name under heaven given to men by which we must be saved" (Acts 4:12).

No other name. No substitute. And it's not Susan or Shirley. It's Jesus! He has all power to do all saving. And he makes salvation available to every person with every name. It's because of his saving power that we have the amazing privilege of becoming his children.

Why pursue holiness? Because we are his. We are his children. We bear his name. And what a magnificent name!

I confess, I'm not very good at remembering names. I might call you Susan. Or Shirley. I might call you Prada, for that matter. But his name I will and must always remember.

Cat-aloging the Names

My kids are funny about names. I wonder if it's some weird psychological response to their mother calling them by the wrong name. They came up with some interesting labels for the stray cat that started hanging around. Someone abandoned a black-and-white tomcat in our neighborhood, and before I knew it we had sort of adopted him. The adoption process was uncontrollably complete when my kids started discussing the name. Once an animal has a name, we seem to have one tough time getting rid of it.

My oldest son wanted to name him "Avenger of Blood" (some of my kids still call him "Vengie" every now and then), but I thought it was a little too disturbing. After some debate, they settled on "Riley."

After a few weeks of putting food and water out for Riley, he started bringing his lady friend around. We're giving them the benefit of the doubt and assuming they were married, because the next thing we knew, Riley's pretty calico sweetheart delivered five bouncing baby kittens in our garage. That was in March. Before we even had an opportunity to get Callie the calico in for her postpartum check up, she was expecting again. On July 10 she gave birth to four more babies. Suddenly we're up to our whiskers in cats!

Callie is definitely taking a trip to the vet. But before I could find homes for the babies, my kids had a meeting to decide on names for them all. No, anything but names! My kids are smart little cookies too. They've figured out through the years that by giving their animals Bible names, their dad and I tend to be suckers when it comes to keeping the little critters. Please don't ask me why. I don't get it either. Nevertheless, they presented the new family members: Abraham, Elijah, Hosea, and Binkie.

Wait a minute, was Binkie a major prophet or a minor prophet? Where did they come up with *Binkie*? They apologized a little for that one, but they said, "What could we do? It fit." It's true. He undoubtedly looked like a Binkie.

I had a little mental picture of instructing a Bible study group to turn in their Bibles to the book of Binkie. That cracked me up. Still, who can argue with a name that fits?

If the Name Fits

God gave Jesus a name that fits in the most magnificent way. It's a name that inspires worship from every created thing. I was in a circle of praying women recently, and as we were praising God, one of them giggled, "God, I almost wish we could stop praising you for a minute, just so we could hear the rocks give you a shout out. Wouldn't that be cool?" Our entire circle of women broke out into praying giggles. But we still simply couldn't stop praising.

His name just has to be exalted, and it's our honor and holy privilege to get to praise that most amazing name. Philippians 2:9–11 says,

> Therefore God exalted him to the highest place
> and gave him the name that is above every name,

that at the name of Jesus every knee should bow,
in heaven and on earth and under the earth,
and every tongue confess that Jesus Christ is Lord,
to the glory of God the Father.

O praise the name of Jesus! When the praise fits, shout it.

And God has given you a name that fits. No "Banana-fanna-fo" with the Father. He calls you by name. He nails it every time. You are his child!

Because we are his children, he is the one we are to always impersonate. "As obedient children." Ephesians 5:1 says, "Therefore be imitators of God [copy Him and follow His example], as well-beloved children [imitate their father]" (AMP). Just as a child imitates the daddy he loves, we are to imitate our heavenly Father.

Out of love for him, let's discover more and more how to imitate his holiness. Surely that's how we should respond to his call. . . . Though I'm not calling you Shirley. And don't call me Susan.

> Do as God does. After all, you are his dear children. Let love be your guide. Christ loved us and offered his life for us as a sacrifice that pleases God. You are God's people, so don't let it be said that any of you are immoral or indecent or greedy. Don't use dirty or foolish or filthy words. Instead, say how thankful you are. Being greedy, indecent, or immoral is just another way of worshiping idols. You can be sure that people who behave in this way will never be part of the kingdom that belongs to Christ and to God.
>
> Don't let anyone trick you with foolish talk. God punishes everyone who disobeys him and says foolish things. So don't have anything to do with anyone like that. You used to be like people living in the dark, but now you are people of the light because you belong to the Lord. So act like people of the light and make your light shine. Be good and honest and truthful, as you try to please the Lord.
>
> Ephesians 5:1–10 CEV

12 Walk Softly and Carry a Gargantuan Purse

We've seen it from the days of Ruth Buzzy's "little old lady in the park" bit on *Laugh-In*—and even before. The purse as a weapon. Even before it held ear-piercing whistles and eye-frying spray containers, a well-wielded purse has long been an effective weapon in and of itself. You can carry a handgun in there if you want, I guess. I say simply walk softly and carry a big honkin' purse.

I love picturing us gals in Rambo mode holding the gargantuan handbag like a semiautomatic weapon, ammo sashed around each shoulder. Instead of your average shells, the holsters would more likely be stuffed with tweezers, ink pens, car keys, and the like. But don't be fooled—the purse is still loaded. At any oncoming threat, we're ready to brandish that danger-to-a-stranger handbag. And those tweezers could pluck a perpetrator's brows within an inch of his fashion life.

One of the trickiest challenges in purse weaponry is to pack the handbag so that it's heavy enough to inflict some damage but not so heavy you can't actually wield it. Some of us have such a purse surplus that there's no way we could manage to swing at anyone or anything without a winch of some kind.

How do you know if your purse is too heavy? Here are the top ten signs:

Top Ten Signs Your Purse Is Too Heavy

1. You can lift the 20-pounders in your handweights class with no problem, but haul your purse around for three minutes and you break out in a total body sweat
2. The shoulder you usually carry it on is about six inches lower than the other one
3. You have to put chalk on your hands before you lift it
4. Your chiropractor releases you to go back to work, but not to carry the purse
5. You have to put wheels on it
6. After you put wheels on it, the highway patrol tickets you for not having it tagged and licensed
7. You've noticed when you're carrying it, every step makes a big *thud*
8. The *thud* is measureable on the Richter Scale
9. The purse needs concrete footings and a more solid foundation
10. It develops its own gravitational pull

I knew I had a problem in the overweight purse department when several people kept mistaking my grey purse for a Greyhound. The bus, not the dog.

A Doggie Bag?

My daughter Allie has a new pup that's nowhere near Greyhound bulk. LuLu is a Pekinese-Poodle-Chihuahua combo—though who ever heard of a Peek-a-poo-hua-hua? From nose to tail it's hardly bigger than a peanut. No kidding, Allie actually has a purse she carries the dog in. It's an entirely different kind of doggie bag.

I'm still amazed at how much the tiny thing can eat. I think it eats its body weight hourly. It's like a teenager. And *what* she eats? That's baffling too. Yesterday she ate part of a pencil, about a quarter of my faux leopard purse, and at least one June bug.

Now personally, I can't imagine looking at my purse and thinking, "My, doesn't that look tasty." Since when is fake leopard "the other white meat"? And I guarantee I have never, *ever* looked at a June bug or two and thought, "Ooh, look, snacks!"

The Bible tells us to crave the right things. Chowing down on God's Word will help us grow in obedience.

> So be done with every trace of wickedness [depravity, malignity] and all deceit and insincerity [pretense, hypocrisy] and grudges [envy, jealousy] and slander and evil speaking of every kind. Like newborn babies you should crave [thirst for, earnestly desire] the pure [unadulterated] spiritual milk, that by it you may be nurtured and grow unto completed salvation.
>
> 1 Peter 2:1–2 AMP

Walking out this life in Christ in the right way has a lot to do with developing the right appetites. We're told to crave the pure milk of the Word. "Pure" food—food for pure, holy living!

Not only is a craving for God's Word a good craving, but it will also help mold our thinking toward purity. It will cause us to hunger after more of the good, pure things in life that will build us up spiritually and encourage us in becoming the fruit-bearing Christ-followers we're meant to be. It keeps us healthy and well-fed.

Oh, how I want to crave those good things that will result in life-fruit! Spiritually delish! That pup? She craves June bugs. I personally find that rather hard to swallow.

Raising My Voice

Speaking of hard to swallow, I had a sore throat a few weeks ago. It wasn't that big of a deal until I lost my voice. The first day I had about 50 percent of it and sounded like I'd swallowed one of LuLu's squeaky toys. After that, I had two entire days of absolutely no voice at all. Nothing. It was so frustrating. I would be trying to communicate something vitally important—you know, like "I'd like a grilled chicken wrap and a Diet Coke, please"—and no one "got me." I tried pantomiming, but you'd be surprised how hard it is to act out "grilled chicken wrap."

"So that's pigs in a blanket, ma'am? No? Turkey maybe?"

More flapping, waving, and assorted gesturing. It was all very "Harpo Marx." But the waitress still didn't get it. She just stared at me like I'd totally lost it. I was waiting for her to come back with, "Would you like a side of medication with that?"

I finally just had to write it down.

I had extra time to think about those kinds of misunderstandings over those no-voice days—since I ordinarily spend such a huge portion of my day talking instead of thinking. As I was writing down instructions for what I wanted to eat, I thought about how God wrote down his instructions too. He gave us the instructions for life, written down in His Word. And it's what he wants us to crave. It's what he desires to feed us. It's what we should carry around for every meal and in every doggie bag. So why do so many of us search for pantomiming, gesturing, and goofy signs from other places instead of just plain reading the Bible? Weird, isn't it?

Psalm 119:5–7 says, "Oh, that my ways were steadfast in obeying your decrees! Then I would not be put to shame when I consider all your commands. I will praise you with an upright heart as I learn your righteous laws."

I want to spend more time raising my voice—especially now that I have one again—in praise to the God who loves us enough to communicate his plans to us plainly.

> O Lord, inspire me more and more every day to love and treasure your Word—to read it, study it, and do it!

I'm asking him to help me to be inspired to holiness by the instructions he's given me, and to help me put those instructions into practice more and more.

And speaking of practice, I could use some extra work on my fowl imitations. Even after I wrote down my lunch order, the waitress still brought me a turkey burger. I stuffed it into my purse to save it for later. The added purse poundage? I chalked it up to extra armament.

> Be strong and very courageous. Be careful to obey all the law my servant Moses gave you; do not turn from it to the right or to the left, that you may be successful wherever you go. Do not let this Book of the Law depart from your mouth; meditate on it day and night, so that you may be careful to do everything written in it. Then you will be prosperous and successful.
>
> Joshua 1:7–8

13 Designer Bags

Why do so many of the cutest purses carry the heftiest price tags? Not long ago I was in a store I knew was over my head. I saw a purse that was absolutely gorgeous. Beautiful, I tell you. I knew I was in trouble, though, when I saw the top-designer name. It was one of those times I was just sure I would turn over that purse price tag and read, "Really, girl, why are you even bothering to look?"

How can you tell a purse is too expensive? If you have to get a second mortgage to buy it or you need to sell one of your children into indentured servitude for a year to close the deal, no doubt it's a bit too pricey. That's when it's more of a "hock-it-book" than a pocketbook. You really do have to look at the numbers.

Math-eze

My son Jordan just finished his first year of college as a math and physics major. Before you ask, the answer is no. He did *not* get the math/physics brain cells from my end of the gene pool. Numbers simply will not float over here. Talk about over my head. I'm a writer. There are only letters. And even the letters are not always necessarily in the right order.

I've heard parents often say that their teens speak a different language. I just never expected that it would be the language of math. I speak English. But while I'm speaking to my teens using letters, words, sentences, and paragraphs, Jordan uses mathspeak. He's speaking in numbers, sums, equations, and other theorem-type words in arithma-language that I totally don't get.

I opened one of his books a few months ago, and it was splattered from one end to the other with symbols and all kinds of Greek code. There were strange signs and ciphers that had to be extraterrestrial. In a few places—and I'm sorry about this—but with all the weird symbols, it looked like the symbols people use to censor profanity. Is there such a thing as math cussing?

It occurred to me that maybe the symbols were just for decoration. Then again, if it was decorative, it certainly wasn't my style. Of course, parents aren't really known for style. Isn't there a formula for that? Parents R Squared?

But while it's an alien décor to me, Jordan loves the math style. I guess number-beauty is in the eye of the beholder.

The Beauty of YOU!

Our own true beauty is in the eye of the Beholder too. Did you know that the Lord God thinks you're beautiful? He loves you—and the love of Christ is ever and always in style. You were designed by The Top Designer of all time. In mathspeak: If *X* equals *LOVE*, then Jesus "*X*'s" *us* times *infinity*. To the greatest power!

First John 3:1–3 (NKJV) says,

> Behold what manner of love the Father has bestowed on us, that we should be called children of God! Therefore the world does not know us, because it did not know Him. Beloved, now we are children of God; and it has not yet been revealed what we shall be, but we know that when He is revealed, we shall be like Him,

> for we shall see Him as He is. And everyone who has this hope in Him purifies himself, just as He is pure.

As his children, we are the recipients of such an amazing inheritance. That moves us to purify ourselves as he is pure, the 1 John passage says. Now there's a definitive equation for holy living!

He loves us so much that he devised a plan to make us his children not just for now but for eternity. That's love! At the moment you gave your life to him, you became his forever child. How marvelous is it that he loves us on every timeline and in every language. As a matter of fact, if there really were such a thing as extraterrestrial hieroglyphs, I have no doubt Jesus would write his love in those too.

Your Love Quotient

Have you ever felt unloved or unimportant? Perhaps since the time you were young, you've continued to feel like the last one chosen when divvying up teams. Have you ever found yourself thinking that God could not possibly love you the same way he does the next gal? Maybe you don't feel as pretty or as clever or anywhere near as lovable as everyone else. Do you ever find yourself wondering if God could really love you—really, truly love *you*?

Don't doubt it for a second, my friend. If we compared you to a designer purse, do you know what number you would find on your price tag? Something on the other side of infinity: the blood of the beloved one-and-only Son of God. Have you given thought to what God the Father was willing to pay for you? Yes, his precious Son! That is what you're worth to him. That's how much he loves you. It's impossible to adequately crunch those numbers.

Our tendency is to find our worth and identity in what we look like. Or what kind of talents we have. Or what we can accomplish. Or what our job title might be. Or what others think of us. Wrong calculations! When we do that, we always have a skewed image of ourselves. We're either frustrated because we'll never be good enough, or we think too highly of ourselves and nullify the work of the grace of God by our pride. Romans 12:3 speaks to that side of the equation when it says, "Do not think of yourself more highly than you ought, but rather think of yourself with sober judgment, in accordance with the measure of faith God has given you."

Tag, You're It!

See yourself as your Father sees you. His precious child? You're it! He sees the Jesus price tag on you and loves you because of your identity in Christ.

Even when Jordan and I aren't speaking the same language, I'm confident he knows how treasured he is to me. He is my son and I love him with all my heart. It boggles my mind (even without numbers) when I consider the fact that my huge love for Jordan is but a fraction of the Father's love for all of us.

Hey, did I say "fraction"? Isn't that a math term? Maybe I can speak a little arithma-language!

> Praise be to the God and Father of our Lord Jesus Christ, who has blessed us in the heavenly realms with every spiritual blessing in Christ. For he chose us in him before the creation of the world to be holy and blameless in his sight. In love he predestined us to be adopted as his sons through Jesus Christ, in accordance with his pleasure and will—to the praise of his glorious grace, which he has freely given us in the One he loves. In him we have redemption through his blood, the

forgiveness of sins, in accordance with the riches of God's grace that he lavished on us with all wisdom and understanding. And he made known to us the mystery of his will according to his good pleasure, which he purposed in Christ, to be put into effect when the times will have reached their fulfillment—to bring all things in heaven and on earth together under one head, even Christ.

In him we were also chosen, having been predestined according to the plan of him who works out everything in conformity with the purpose of his will, in order that we, who were the first to hope in Christ, might be for the praise of his glory.

Ephesians 1:3–12

---

14 Purse-onification

I mentioned the fright of looking into my purse and having it look back. But I've discovered that a lot of women have more than just a face tucked inside those scary handbags. Terrifying though it is, I've seen purses that unquestionably carried additional body parts. I think I've seen a high percentage of an entire person in some of them. It gives personification (or purse-sonification) a whole new implication when, with the right strike of lightning, a purse could get up and walk. Frankenpurse lives!

Hairpieces, gloves, fake lashes, and foot potions. Head and shoulders, knees and toes, knees and toes. And don't forget the nails!

Nailing Down a Knack for Listening

While we're "touching" on nails, here's a little piece of advice: never scrimp on fake fingernails. If you've ever picked up a set of those mega-cheap ones when you were in a nail pinch, no doubt you completely understand what I'm talking about. How awkward is it to have one of those slippery little rascals flick across a room? Have you ever nailed someone upside the head? Now that's embarrassing. But it's the absolute worst when you're at a fancy event, smiling uncomfortably with your face redder than the most crimson nail polish as you're picking a rogue nail out of some stranger's salad. No, wait. Actually, the absolute worst would be if the stranger ate the salad before you got to it.

Isn't it mind-boggling that so many women who are caught fishing through strangers' salads were in fact warned about the wayward nails beforehand (as in, "before" applying them to the "hand")? Why don't they listen?

In the book of Zechariah, the Lord had told his people to be truthful and just, merciful and compassionate, to take care of each other, take care of strangers, and to think the best about each other. Did they listen? Did they obey? Nope. Zechariah 7:13 is probably one of the saddest verses in Scripture: " 'When I called, they did not listen; so when they called, I would not listen,' says the Lord Almighty."

Could it be any plainer? When he calls and we refuse to listen, then we will call and he will refuse to listen. Judgment comes when we won't listen. Obedience for the child of God is not an option. And those who don't listen will undoubtedly get nailed in the worst way. There are always consequences when we choose to disobey.

How Do We Tune In?

Let's continually tune in to the most practical ways to listen to God. We learn his commands and how he wants us to manage our lives and our minds by reading his Word. We obey him when we do what it says. We stay connected to him through prayer and being in tune with his Holy Spirit at work in our lives, and we respond when the Holy Spirit convicts us of any sin that pops up.

Refusing to listen is as foolish as wearing the worst nails to the nicest dinner. In Deuteronomy 30:19–21 we're reminded that choosing to listen to God our Father is choosing life. "Love the LORD your God, listen to his voice, and hold fast to him. For the LORD is your life" (vv. 20–21).

The secret to listening and obeying? Making sure the Lord is our *life*. The pursuit of holiness is wrapped up in being consumed with him, in recognizing that he is our life, and in loving him and desiring to obey him with every ounce of heart and soul.

Deuteronomy 30:10 recaps that thought alongside the "big if": "If you obey the LORD your God and keep his commands and decrees that are written in this Book of the Law and turn to the LORD your God with all your heart and with all your soul." Verse 9 says that heeding the "big if" will delight the Lord and make us prosperous. Who wouldn't love to delight him with a prosperous soul?

Reach for the Sky

Are you thinking it's just too hard? God anticipated that. Before the people could even voice it, he told them in verses 11–14,

> Now what I am commanding you today is not too difficult for you or beyond your reach. It is not up in heaven, so that you have to ask, "Who will ascend into heaven to get it and proclaim it to us so we may obey it?" Nor is it beyond the sea, so that you have to ask, "Who will cross the sea to get it and proclaim it to us so we may obey it?" No, the word is very near you; it is in your mouth and in your heart so you may obey it.

He'll never ask us to do something that's out of our reach. He puts the ability to listen and obey right in our hearts—he said so! As we listen and obey the Spirit of God, we're reaching toward that holy obedience. Hot pursuit!

We're pursuing holiness and showing love to our Father when we're obediently listening and holding on to him, just as verse 20 conveys it: "Love the Lord your God, listen to his voice, and hold fast to him." Hold on to him with the tightest grip, and you're pursuing holiness, even if you don't know it!

Nails with Bite

And speaking of holding on with the tightest grip, be careful with that nail glue when you're clandestinely trying to repair one of those cheap nails under the table. I once accidentally glued my finger to a shrimp fork. Talk about a tight grip.

Of course, for some the fake nails are the answer to an addiction. I heard about a lady who decided to kick the nail-biting habit. She told her husband that she planned to do it by getting some press-on nails. He said, "Oh yeah, great idea. It'll save you time. You can snack on those right out of the box."

I wonder if he knows they're just as good sprinkled on your favorite salad.

> Now it shall come to pass, when all these things come upon you, the blessing and the curse which I have set before you, and you call them to mind among all the nations where the LORD your God drives you, and you return to the LORD your God and obey His voice, according to all that I command you today, you and your children, with all your heart and with all your soul, that the LORD your God will bring you back from captivity, and have compassion on you, and gather you again from all the nations where the LORD your God has scattered you. If any of you are driven out to the farthest parts under heaven, from there the LORD your God will gather you, and from there He will bring you. Then the LORD your God will bring you to the land which your fathers possessed, and you shall possess it. He will prosper you and multiply you more than your fathers. And the LORD your God will circumcise your heart and the heart of your descendants, to love the LORD your God with all your heart and with all your soul, that you may live. Also the LORD your God will put all these curses on your enemies and on those who hate you, who persecuted you. And you will again obey the voice of the LORD and do all His commandments which I command you today.
>
> Deuteronomy 30:1–8 NKJV

In My Grandma's Handbag 15

My grandma's purse was the purse of a real woman. It always fascinated me when I was a little girl. It smelled different—mostly like Vicks, to be specific. Grandma was sure that Vicks could cure just about anything. And anything not quite appropriate for the Vicks-fix would get the Campho-phenique treatment. Her purse was an aroma-rama in eucalyptus and camphor. One good sniff into Grandma's purse could clear your sinuses for a week.

Grandma's purse looked different on the outside too. She liked nice things but didn't worry so much if the bag matched the shoes—or if either was completely in style, for that matter. She was her own trendsetter. She made her own style. Grandma was a woman comfortable in her own purse-fashion world.

My grandma's purse was sturdy and practical—and hefty. Hers was a purse you could really sink your teeth into. And since I mentioned it, there was one time I literally saw my grandma slip her teeth into her purse. It really was a purse you could sink your teeth into.

Grandma's purse was a purse of maturity. I had a great deal of respect for my grandma's handbag. It carried safety pins and needle and thread, so she had you covered for just about any clothing emergency. You could always find a hanky in there too. Not paper. No, it was real cloth. Wrinkled with a few lipstick stains, but real cloth. Mind you, I still have a reflex cringe when I see one of those wrinkled hankies. It's because I can still picture my grandma swirling it over her tongue, then coming at some smudge on my face with the dreaded spittle-hankie. But I always knew the slobber-hankie was pulled out of her purse in love.

My grandma was ready-at-the-purse with a stick of Dentyne for anyone anytime a gum-need hit. And you'd best not mention her grandkids if you didn't want her dragging that little album of pictures out of that handbag. She was ever-ready with that too. If a purse can be filled with love, Grandma's was.

Am I Carrying a "Big Girl" Bag?

When I was a girl, every once in a while I compared my purse with Grandma's. No comparison, really. Grandma's had everything practical in it. Mine had wax lips in it. Hers had a sturdy leather-look plastic strap on it. Mine had a picture of Tinkerbell on it.

My purse has matured over the years. It may not measure up to Grandma's, but at least I hardly ever carry wax lips anymore. I think I've grown into a "big girl" purse.

I have to keep a close check on living the "big girl" life. It's easy to slip back into immature thoughts and actions. Maturing spiritually means we stop thinking that God has to first sort of "bribe" us with blessings for us to obey. "Do this for me or that for my family, Lord, and I will do this and such for you." What a Tinkerbell prayer. Part of growing up spiritually means that I no longer obey, love, serve, and pursue holiness with a giant "if" attached to it. It means I must obey, love, serve, and pursue holiness with a giant "whatever" attached to it instead.

We can't hold our obedience or our service for ransom. When we do that, we're pursuing blessings, not holiness. If I want to become more and more the child of God he wants me to be, I need to give him a mature "whatever" when it comes to obedience.

The "Whatever" Life

When my daughter Kaley was fourteen, we had a big decision to make for her related to her schooling. Kaley is a real talker. I have no idea where she gets that. She's funny and articulate, but even though she's quite the conversationalist, she sometimes has a tough time telling me what's truly on her mind about the most serious things. She's as ready with a quip as Grandma was with the Vicks, but trying to find out what's going on in her head and heart can sometimes be tricky.

I told Kaley I was losing sleep over that big school decision because I knew she wasn't really going to like the decision her dad and I thought was best for her. All along the way, I really wanted her input. I wanted to know what she was feeling. But every time

I asked, about all I got was, "Whatever." It was the same answer I got when we were deciding which fast-food restaurant to drive through. "Whatever."

Then one evening I found this note on my pillow:

Dear Mom,

I just wanted to tell you what a great job you're doing. You really are. You are probably one of the most loving people I have ever met. You always want to know what I'm thinking. You always want what's best for me and the others. I hope there's no doubt in your mind what a wonderful mother you really are.

I am just filled with joy whenever I think of what a unique and beautiful person God gave me to call "Mom," especially when I see other mothers and daughters fighting with each other. I don't think we've ever really screamed at each other, even when we disagree, it's never too bad, and before we know it, a funny joke or a silly look has us laughing and just being buds again. Just your presence in my life is always a comfort, and I really want you to understand that.

You just fill so many roles for me in my life: mother, mentor, friend, confidante, and also my hero. I know I don't tell you these things enough, but just because I don't always know how to say things doesn't mean I don't feel them for you, Mom.

I know you get frustrated with me when I say "whatever" to you. I'm just not good at talking about what I'm feeling or thinking. I can talk about what other people are feeling and thinking all day, but I don't always know how to do it myself. But you need to know that "whatever" doesn't mean that I don't care or that it doesn't matter to me. It means that I trust you. I know that whatever we do, you will be doing what is best for me, whether it's where to eat dinner, or more important things.

I want you to be at peace knowing that whatever decisions you may come to at any time concerning me, I trust you. I may not always agree, and I may not always like your decision, but I trust you.

So don't be discouraged when I say frustrating things like "whatever" in answer to some of your questions. In Kaley-ese [that is, of course, the language of the Kaley] it means that I know you love me and that I'm not concerned about you making the right decision.

You know, I may never get to a point where I can actually articulate that stuff. You know, out loud. Like I said, anybody else's problems or feelings, and I'm just fine, just don't ask me about mine. Well, if I ever have to go to a psychiatrist or something, he may never figure me out, but at least when he asks me about my mother I'll be able to give him rave reviews.

Completely Sincerely,
Kaley Faith Rhea

P.S. I want you to get some sleep now. Don't worry.

Is that the sweetest thing ever (and yes, she really did sign it with her full name)? To say that her note blessed me is the understatement of the decade. I was in a total puddle—somewhere near the fetal position, I think. I've read it many times in the last couple of years (she's now seventeen), but I don't know if I've ever been able to read it completely tear-free. She so blessed me and honored me with her sweet trust.

I learn so much from my children about my relationship with my heavenly Father. I want to honor him that way. I want to let him know he's my hero. I want to be able to say to him at anytime, anywhere, about anything: "Whatever." *Whatever you want me to do, Lord. Whatever you want me to say. Whatever you want me to be. Whatever you want me to experience. I may not always agree, and I may not always like your decision, but I trust you. Whatever decisions you may come to at any time concerning me—I know you love me and I trust you, Lord.*

The "whatever" life, my friend, is the life of holiness.

You may have been just at the threshold many times of making that decision to obey him completely, to depend on him and to give him your "whatever." How many times have you been oh so close, just to step back? How many times have you convinced yourself that if you took that step in complete surrender, God would surely pack you up and send you off to the darkest, most bug-infested jungles where you would pout your life away without air-conditioning or sidewalks—or even Vicks or Dentyne?

Do you really think our heavenly Father wants or needs a pouting servant? He doesn't. Get your heart ready to go or do or be "whatever," but understand that he won't call you without equipping you from the heart out. He wants your trust as much as he wants your "whatever."

We must bow before him "as obedient children"—that's our call. Our call to the holy life is a call of complete surrender. It's all about a life surrendered in love. Our "whatever" should be as filled with love as Grandma's purse—a love that overflows in obedience. Toss away that Tinkerbell/Peter Pan "never gonna grow up" kind of thinking, and take a step of maturity in your pursuit of the holy life.

Never Gonna Grow Up

Being his child doesn't mean I should stay immature any more than I should still be carrying around wax lips as an adult. Yes, God's Word does say to come as a little child—with childlike trust and obedience and abandon. But we're not called to *stay* babies. We're called to grow up and be holy. Remember 1 Corinthians 13:11: "When I was a child, I spoke and thought and reasoned as a child does. But when I grew up, I put away childish things" (NLT[a]).

Just as a healthy person grows physically, a healthy Christian grows spiritually. When you're confronted with the topic of those baby issues, does something in particular pop into your mind? Is there an area where you have no doubt you need to grow in holiness? Are you ready to give him your "whatever"?

The "whatever" life is an exciting journey. You're going to love the wild ride! If you get a little schmutz on you along the way, no worries. I'm stuffing a hankie in my purse.

> Then we will no longer be infants, tossed back and forth by the waves, and blown here and there by every wind of teaching and by the cunning and craftiness of men in their deceitful scheming. Instead, speaking the truth in love, we will in all things grow up into him who is the Head, that is, Christ. From him the whole body, joined and held together by every supporting ligament, grows and builds itself up in love, as each part does its work. . . .
>
> You were taught, with regard to your former way of life, to put off your old self, which is being corrupted by its deceitful desires; to be made new in the attitude of your minds; and to put on the new self, created to be like God in true righteousness and holiness.
>
> Ephesians 4:14–16, 22–24

Part 4

"Do not conform to the evil desires you had when you lived in ignorance"

16

That's a Purse of a Different Color

I saw a purse that was advertized as "the purse for every occasion." It was one handy-dandy handbag, alright. But only one purse for all occasions? Can't picture it. I do have a friend who is a one-purse woman. She remains faithful to one bag until the zipper is rusted and the lining turns to powder. But in my mind, there's surely a different kind of purse for every kind of event. Every purse has its party and every party has its purse.

So many purses in the world—what a waste it would be if we each only needed one. We've all seen purses in all sizes, shapes, and colors—and even colors that are so different, they're almost not quite legally considered colors. I once had a taupe purse that looked purple in just the right light, then appeared to be some kind of mustardy-brown color in just the wrong light. Ugly but interesting.

Still, the purse-of-many-colors idea has definite possibilities. How about a purse that changes colors? Wouldn't it be fun to see a "mood purse" hit the market? *"Don't go near Doris today. Get a load of that bag. Midnight blue."* Or *"Today's the day I'm asking for that raise. It's the boss's pink purse day."*

Instead of a mood purse, I tend to go with more of a "different purse for every mood" approach. With as many emotions as I can carry around, that could call for a boatload of purses. I hope the boat is actually a cruise ship. I have a purse for that.

But exactly how can we know when enough purses is too many?

Top Ten Ways to Know You Have Too Many Purses

1. When you go on vacation, you have to carry an entire bag of bags
2. You're forced to put a "wide load" banner on the bag of bags and have escort vehicles drive before and behind your car
3. You've had to pare down to three outfits so you'll have more purse space in your closet
4. Your husband gives you the okay to build on that spa room, but you opt for building additional purse storage instead
5. You have more purses than Baskin Robbins has flavors
6. You have more purses than Baskin Robbins has calories
7. You decide to develop a schedule so you'll have a different purse for each day, then you realize your present inventory will carry you into the year 3023
8. You realize you could also supply a purse a day for your entire ladies' Bible study group through the year 3023
9. The purses have banded together and formed their own union
10. The purse section of your closet has its own time zone

Time to do a little purse sorting (whatever the time zone)? I've already admitted that for me, the "boatload of purses" ship has already sailed.

Passing On the Pink Purse Passion

All purse-hoarding issues aside, the portion of the 1 Peter passage that compels us not to "conform to the evil desires" spurs us on in our holy pursuit. Hanging on to a few extra purses is one thing. But hanging on to the old way of life when we've been made completely new? That's no way to live. That's living in the "Midnight Blue" mood-zone when a perfect "pink purse day" is right there for the grabbing. Why live the blue-blasé way when we can have a life of perpetual pink-tinted passion instead?

How we choose to pursue holiness affects not only our own mood, but it also affects the lives of all those around us as well. What kind of inspiration to live holy lives are we passing on to our friends and our families? What are we passing on to our children? As a mother, I can tell you, you are not likely to see your children naturally pursuing a holy life if you aren't pursuing a holy life yourself.

We're called to live a life that is holy—set apart—one that mirrors Jesus. When people look at our lives, they should be able to see Christ. Do people see Jesus when they look at your life, or is there an old sin habit that's hindering your pursuit of holiness?

Titus 3:3 says, "Once we, too, were foolish and disobedient. We were misled and became slaves to many lusts and pleasures. Our lives were full of evil and envy, and we hated each other" (NLT[a]). Paul describes a life that's all about selfishness and sin. Not pretty.

But that was the old life.

Getting Rid of Old Baggage

It's time to put away those old ways. In contrast to the purse issues, we need to get rid of any of that old sin baggage. Giving our lives to Christ brings a new Spirit-filled way of life. The Titus passage continues,

> But—"When God our Savior revealed his kindness and love, he saved us, not because of the righteous things we had done, but because of his mercy. He washed away our sins, giving us a new birth and new life through the Holy Spirit. He generously poured out the Spirit upon us through Jesus Christ our Savior. Because of his grace he declared us righteous and gave us confidence that we will inherit eternal life." This is a trustworthy saying, and I want you to insist on these teachings so that all who trust in God will devote themselves to doing good. These teachings are good and beneficial for everyone.
>
> Titus 3:4–8 NLT[b]

Notice it's not only beneficial for you and I to understand these teachings, but the teachings are "good and beneficial for everyone." Let's pass them on! We can do that as we "trust in God" and as we're devoted "to doing good" and as we lead others in the holiness pursuit. And actually, that's pursuing holiness and inspiring others to pursue holiness at the very same time.

I love that thought. As a matter of fact, if I had a mood purse, it would be glowing the most glorious pink right now!

> If anyone belongs to Christ, there is a new creation. The old things have gone; everything is made new! All this is from God. Through Christ, God made peace between us and himself, and God gave us the work of telling everyone about the peace we can have with him. God was in Christ, making peace between the world and himself. In Christ, God did not hold the world guilty of its sins. And he gave us this message of peace. So we have been sent to speak for Christ. It is as if God is calling to you through us. We speak for Christ when we beg you to be

at peace with God. Christ had no sin, but God made him become sin so that in Christ we could become right with God.

2 Corinthians 5:17–21 NCV[b]

17 This Bag Is *Smokin'*!

I've noticed a lot of electrical activity coming from purses these days. There's a new kind of disturbance in the purse force. Major leaps in purse-sized technology! Cell phones were just the beginning. Now we have purse-sized computers, TVs, and every kind of music-making device—just about every techno-gadget you can imagine is in that purse.

Hey, I remember when a Blackberry was a fruit! There's been a purse-sized technological revolution. And while the technology may vary from purse to purse, it's difficult to find any bag anywhere that's not wired for something measured in volts or megahertz.

I think I might've seen a handbag the other day that was wired for *cable.* That seemed a little excessive to me, but I would still definitely consider a big voltage battery purse pack. Or maybe I should just figure out a way to wire my bag for its own outlet. A purse with a plug in!

Knowing how I deal with electrical issues, I have no doubt that if I tried to hot-wire a purse, I would end up flying across the room and then thrashing around in an attempt to get my bangs to stop smoking. It's hard to relax and enjoy playing senseless purse video games when you know that at any moment your bag could burst into flame and you could be forced to throw your body on it in some kind of stop, drop, and roll move.

It's All in Your Head

Dealing with electrical issues is still probably not as shocking as the realization of how many changes we often need to make to head down a holy path. Struggling with how to change unholy behavior? I'm sincere when I tell you that most of it is in your head. To change our behavior, we have to change our thinking. Just as our focal passage in 1 Peter told us to prepare our minds for action, we prepare for behavior action in our minds. We touched on the gathering of the robes, getting ready to act. We need to gather our thoughts and get them ready for the right kind of action. Changing your behavior starts with what's happening in your head.

In Matthew 22:37 Jesus said, "You shall love the Lord your God with all your heart, with all your soul, and with all your mind" (NKJV). We truly want to love Jesus with our behavior—with our entire life and our entire being. Why do we so often try to leave out the mind? There it is in black and white. We're instructed to love him with all our "mind."

It's easy to convince ourselves that everything that happens in the secret places of our gray matter doesn't count. But thinking it through, we understand that what happens in the secret places of our mind determines our actions.

In many ways, you are what you think. Your thoughts will make the difference between a holy walk and an unholy one. Reel in those thoughts. Gather them up. Bring them to Jesus and let him change your way of thinking! That's the way to live holy. Think differently. "Don't copy the behavior and customs of this world, but let God transform you into a new person by changing the way you think. Then you will learn to know God's will for you, which is good and pleasing and perfect" (Romans 12:2 NLT[b]).

It's How We're Wired

Wiring is important. We all know I'm the last person you'd want wiring a purse for an outlet. I'm the last person you'd want wiring *anything*, truth be told. I once played around with a cute little old lamp. Nothing fancy. Just an old lamp with some old wiring. But before I knew it, I saw sparks and a hint of smoke. I jerked the plug out of the wall somewhere just this side of major combustion.

In my defense, it really was an old lamp. I should've known that to have the electricity flow through it safely, that old wiring would need to be replaced.

Isn't that how it is in life sometimes? We have to rip out the old before we can plug in the new. If we want holiness to flow from our lives and if we want a mind that's ready for pursuing the holy life, we have to be willing to rip out the old way of thinking, replacing our thoughts (wrapped up in that old way of doing things) with God's thoughts (his high and holy thinking). There is no holy walk, and there will be no sweet fellowship with our holy God without changing the way we think.

Ready for new wiring? Paul helps us jumpstart the rewiring of the mind in Philippians 4:8 (AMP) when he says,

> Whatever is true, whatever is worthy of reverence and is honorable and seemly, whatever is just, whatever is pure, whatever is lovely and lovable, whatever is kind and winsome and gracious, if there is any virtue and excellence, if there is anything worthy of

praise, think on and weigh and take account of these things—fix your minds on them.

Think About It

Let's spark some thought—the good kind of nonflammable spark. We're essentially instructed here to *give thought to our thoughts*. We need to keep a tight rein on our thinking. Are there patterns of thinking we catch ourselves indulging in that lead us down an unholy path? Time to get out the thought extinguisher!

Paul doesn't merely instruct us to rip out the old wires—that old selfish, worldly, sinful way of thinking—and then leave us there sort of "thoughtless." No, he tells us how to rewire with new thinking. We're told what kinds of thoughts should replace the old ones. We're told to rewire with thoughts that are true, respectable and right, pure, full of love, kind, gracious, virtuous, praiseworthy—good things. That's the kind of thinking we're to "fix" our minds on.

And "fix" our minds it does! Replacing the old thoughts with Jesus-thinking truly is the fix. It's the repair of all repairs—nothing like my lamp work. His fix even works *without* an outlet. After all, he is the Source, the God of all power.

Power Suit

Speaking of power, I experienced it on a small scale a few Sundays ago when I wore my bright red power suit to church. I'm not even the one who dubbed it my "power suit"—one of my friends did—but I have to admit, I liked it. Wearing a power suit made me want to do something . . . well . . . powerful. If the suit had a cape, I might've tried to fly.

I was pondering something powerful to do during the song service and, wouldn't you know it, the electricity went out. No sound system. No electric guitar. Our piano is electric too. We had drums and that was about it. There we were without power while I was sitting on the front row in my power suit. Seems like I should've been able to plug that thing in somewhere, doesn't it? All that red-suit power—and it was useless for the song service.

You know what's really funny? We didn't need my red-suit power. We didn't even need the electrical power. God's power showed up despite the lack of electricity. He didn't need the piano or the sound system. Without any of those things, we had a wonderfully powerful time of worship.

Where does real power come from? It comes from the Lord. His power will show up for you too. Let me say it in the most powerful way: He don't need no power suit! The more our minds are renewed and rewired, the more we understand the great and wondrous power there is in his name. Jeremiah 10:6 exclaims, "Lord, there is no one like you! For you are great, and your name is full of power" (NLT[b]). Power in the suit? No, power in his name!

Go ahead. Rewire your mind and plug into the power he provides. AC/DC—doesn't matter. There's not a voltage he doesn't have covered.

And by the way, if there's ever smoke, it will always be the good, holy kind. Yes, holy smoke.

> I appeal to you therefore, brethren, and beg of you in view of all the mercies of God, to make a decisive dedication of your bodies presenting all your members and faculties as a living sacrifice, holy, devoted, consecrated and well pleasing to God, which is your reasonable, rational, intelligent service and spiritual worship. Do not be

conformed to this world, this age, fashioned after and adapted to its external, superficial customs, but be transformed, changed by the entire renewal of your mind by its new ideals and its new attitude, so that you may prove for yourselves what is the good and acceptable and perfect will of God, even the thing which is good and acceptable and perfect in His sight for you.

Romans 12:1–2 AMP

18 Purse Burps—and Other Embarrassing Discombobulations

Back in the baby days, it was always tough to know exactly where the purse started and the diaper bag left off—and vice versa. Somewhere by the fourth or fifth baby, the two bags had begun to morph into a one bag with two identities—and troubled identities at that. Yes, rather schizoid bags, I'm afraid.

As a matter of fact, I remember once loading all the kids into the car for church and getting myself buckled, too, before realizing I had a can of hairspray in my hand. I had all five of my kids within seven years, so back then, by the time I got everyone into all their various car seats and boosters with buckles, I did *not* want to go back into the house. No going back. So the hairspray had to go into the diaper bag. It was a little tough to explain to the nursery workers at church that I really wasn't expecting them to style my babies.

And it went both ways. I once stuffed the baby powder in my purse. The problem with that move became all too apparent when

I was out with a group of women at a restaurant and squeezed my purse in just the wrong way. Not a problem if the twisty powder cap is turned in the right direction. But who remembers to twist the cap? The holes were completely unobstructed and the entire purse gave a huge white burp. Talk about difficult to explain.

"Excuse me" doesn't begin to cut it.

Learning the Labels

Eventually, I had to learn to put baby things in the diaper bag, grown-up things (mostly) in my purse. Although the babies are mostly teens, I will admit that even now I still find a little truck wheel now and then. I admit, too, that there were countless times I stuffed the wrong thing in the wrong place. And I can't say that the restaurant purse burp was the only time I had a white cloud over my purse. I'm just glad my purse never fully developed its own baby powder atmosphere.

Maybe I should've tried labeling everything. The baby powder would've definitely had a "diaper bag" label. But then my kids were always tucking things in one bag or another when I wasn't looking. How was I supposed to label my eight-year-old's bottle cap collection? And while we're asking questions, why did he feel the need to stick it in my purse? And what about that rubber chicken I found in the diaper bag? What kind of label would I put on that? I mean really, where is the proper place for a rubber chicken?

Sometimes we really don't know what we're carrying. Imagine the look on my face at the grocery store when I reached for my billfold and pulled out a rubber chicken instead. And while we're imagining, imagine the checker's face. "Um, we only take cash, check, or credit card."

Your rubber chicken. Don't leave home without it.

I'm not the only one who carries little surprises. I heard about a National Guardsman who was coming on duty at the airport. He had to go through the metal detector like everyone else. He handed his rifle to the airport security person, but he still beeped on his way through the metal detector. He finally realized that his little nail clipper was the culprit. Surprise. It was deep inside one of his pockets, and he had totally forgotten he had it. Of course, how funny did it look when the security folks took his clippers, telling him they were prohibited, then handed him back his M-16.

Time to Learn What We're Putting Where

Learning to make holy choices is vital—it's a spiritual way of putting on the right labels and putting the right things into the right places. Ready to learn? Ephesians 5:17 says, "So do not be foolish but learn what the Lord wants you to do" (NCV[a]).

I might as well tell you that sometimes learning is gloriously pleasant, but sometimes it can be downright painful—especially in the area of sin. But not learning? That's so much more painful.

Learning should result in change. And our learning should always be based in God's truth. Since his truth never changes, we need to be the ones doing the changing. We change in response to the lessons he teaches us by his truth. And when we refuse to learn those lessons the first time, guess what? We have to go another round. We're doomed to repeat the same mistakes until we accept his truth and change according to it.

It was embarrassing enough to pull out a rubber chicken the first time. But how goofy would I have looked the second time it happened? Or the third?

How it must break the heart of God when we're slow to learn spiritual lessons—when we're so slow to obey. How often do we turn back to that old way, conforming to the evil desires we had when we lived in ignorance?

Are you ready to commit to learning whatever your Father wants you to learn? Are you ready to choose obedience? Are you ready to commit to right choices? Ask the Lord to open your eyes to the old paths of sin. Sometimes those old paths are well-worn and easy to slip back onto. Ask him to give you the wisdom to choose well. That's how we can arm ourselves for the holy life in all the right ways. We don't need an M-16—not even a nail clipper. He'll provide everything we need to choose holiness.

Label Makers

My daughter Kaley and I like to write together, but we've gotten stuck on labels a time or two. We're not always the best label makers, I guess. We were polishing a fiction story line several months ago. I glanced at the clock and told her that we still had a few plot snags we needed to iron out and we didn't have much time. "No, wait," I said. "You can't 'iron out' a 'snag.' That's a total mix of fabric metaphors."

Kaley came back with, "Yeah, but what do you do with a snag?"

"I think it might depend on the percentage of polyester. But if it's a snag on a sweater you can usually pull it through to the back side." Okay, that didn't help.

"Sometimes we snip them with scissors, don't we?" Kaley offered.

We discussed other options for proper snag disposition for the next several minutes. "Doesn't matter," she finally said. "We're not going to pull the story line to the back side and I can't see us snipping it either. I don't care how much polyester is in this thing, if we need to iron it out, then it's going to need to be a plot wrinkle instead of a plot snag."

"Yeah, that's it! Let's iron out the plot wrinkles." Boy, did it feel great to find just the right label for the plot wrinkle. Until I started feeling stupid. I felt like a real dork because we'd spent fifteen minutes of the time we didn't really have labeling our plot wrinkles instead of ironing them out. Oh, the irony! (Get it? *Iron-y?*)

I wonder how much of our lives we waste labeling things that we really should just plain get rid of. We spend time trying to decide if that was really a lie or if it was just a bit of an exaggeration. Were we being impatient and unkind, or were we just a little tired? Was that really a sinful desire or just a random thought no one needs to know about?

When it comes to sin, we need to label it what it really is: sin. First John 1:8–9 says, "If we say we have no sin, we are only fooling ourselves and refusing to accept the truth. But if we confess our sins to him, he is faithful and just to forgive us and to cleanse us from every wrong" (NLT[a]). Let's make sure we're not trying to turn in the nail clippers while hanging on to the M-16—or even the other way around. If it's sin, it needs to go.

Coming face to face with our sin can be pretty ugly. But it's what we need to do to be able to bury that sin and move on to the holy places God has called us to. When we confess our sins, God forever removes those sin wrinkles in the most wonderful "permanent press" kind of way. *The Message* phrases Romans 8:12–14 this way: "So don't you see that we don't owe this old do-it-yourself life one red cent. There's nothing in it for us, nothing at all. The best thing to do is give it a decent burial and get on with your new life. God's Spirit beckons. There are things to do and places to go!"

Press On

Learning to immediately confess sin instead of labeling it or excusing it will help us move on to those "things to do and places to go." In your own holy pursuit, let me encourage you to keep *pressing on*!

And while we're learning, it's good to learn a few labeling lessons. A puff of white powder belching itself out of your purse could probably get you arrested in some circles. A rightly placed "baby powder" label might just keep you out of jail.

> I have restrained my feet from every evil way, that I might keep Your word, hearing, receiving, loving, and obeying it. I have not turned aside from Your ordinances, for You Yourself have taught me. How sweet are Your words to my taste, sweeter than honey to my mouth! Through Your precepts I get understanding; therefore I hate every false way.
>
> Psalm 119:101–4 AMP

19

I Found My Purse, Now Where Are My Keys?

I think I've lost my purse in just about every state of the union. It's almost criminal that this absentminded person should be allowed to carry around a handbag with assorted valuables, credit information, and other vital statistics. Even at home, when I schedule time to get ready to leave the house, I have to schedule time for showering, dressing, hair, and makeup, yes. But I also have to set aside at least twenty minutes for the purse search.

There's usually about ten minutes of looking high and low, ten minutes of looking over and under, then I end up finding it in some weird place I'd never expect. Like the fridge. Incidentally, scatterbrained people should avoid snacking while holding a purse.

As terrible as I am about misplacing my purse, I'm even worse about my keys. Maybe it's because they're so much smaller. That means there are lots more of those tiny, remote spaces they can hide. It doesn't matter how many times we designate one particular spot the "key place," the keys never seem to end up anywhere near there. Of course, the most embarrassing place to find the keys is . . . hanging from the front door. I hate that. Every time.

Some people say keys jingle. Not mine. After I finally find them and grab them up from their sneaky little hiding place, they snicker. Sinisterly. And it's all the more warped that they love to play their annoying game of hide-and-seek when I'm already half an hour late and I need to lock up and leave. I can just picture the rascals tiptoeing outside just before I'm ready to go so they can hang themselves from the door.

I've been trying to set a goal to keep a closer eye on my purse and my keys, but I've yet to nail anything down. I think I heard the keys chuckling just yesterday.

Aim for Nothing and You'll Likely Hit It

In other more worthy goals, chapter 2 mentioned setting holy goals and setting them high. That's one huge way you can guard against conforming "to the evil desires you had when you lived in ignorance."

Just as I can't drive my car until I find my keys, often setting goals is "key" in giving us the "drive" to achieve spiritual success. Have you been going nowhere in your pursuit of holiness? Maybe it's time to grab the keys and get your spiritual engines revved up by mapping out your holy pursuit more specifically.

We're much more likely to hit what we're aiming for if we're actually aiming for something. How fruitless is target practice without a target? Do you ever find yourself feeling like you're not accomplishing anything? Do you bounce from one project to another, not finishing any? Girlfriend, it happens to me all the time. I notice myself giving in to every distraction and accomplishing nothing, then I get to the end of the day and feel like a total loser. And when it happens to me, I know it's time to either go back and look at my life goals, or it's time to set some new ones.

Our One True Goal

We have one goal in common. It's the banner goal of giving glory to God that flies over all the rest and ties them all together in eternal purpose. What is our ultimate goal? Holiness. We want to look like Jesus. What kind of goals will help us hit our holy bull's-eye?

Underneath our banner goal of holiness should be specific sub-goals—the goals that help us continually move toward that one true goal. Once you understand the target, the distractions are much more easily sorted out of your day, and they lose their power to rob you of your fruitfulness. You ask yourself as you introduce each new activity, "Does this help me hit one of the goals that will make me look more like Jesus?"

It's easy to let busyness take over our day. We end up burned out when we're spinning our wheels on the frivolous activities that don't get us any closer to our most worthwhile goals. Even in church work, we can get so busy working *for* the Lord that we forget our number one goal of becoming *like* the Lord—holy.

Purse-onalize Your Goals

Need some goal suggestions? Here are a few to get you started. Under each goal you should list detailed, solid actions you need to take to help keep you on the path of your overall goal. Personalize them; make them applicable to you. Don't shoot for something ambiguous. Make your goals precise and real. If you write them out to fit your own personal objectives, you'll have something tangible you can look to that will help you revalidate your goals any time you need extra direction.

1. God's Word transforms our thinking, clarifying our number one goal. Read it every day. Study it. Memorize it. Let it become part of your thinking.
2. Pray every day. Ask God to make you holy. Desire it. Thirst for it. Spend time praising and worshiping him, as well as asking him to meet your needs. You become like those whose company you keep. Keep company with Jesus. Time with him daily is absolutely essential to your growth in holiness.
3. Since you become like those whose company you keep, spend time with people who encourage you in your pursuit of holiness. Is there someone in your life who loves Jesus in a way that inspires you? After you've been with this person, is your desire to be more like Christ? Set a goal to spend time with that person, strengthening your holiness

pursuit. Make yourself accountable to someone in any areas of weakness.

4. Become a person who motivates another to pursue holiness. You'll be inspired in your own pursuit of holiness as you see yourself encouraging a sister to be holy and to love Jesus more.
5. In addition to encouraging others to grow, serve the Lord in at least one very planned, very concrete way.
6. Serve him through a local body of believers. Be connected, active, and giving of yourself—giving your time, your talents, and your resources. The church is part of God's plan for you. Make it part of your plan for him.
7. Set work goals and financial goals that reflect what is truly important to your Father. Show by your actions that the things that are important to God are the things that are important to you.

As you're setting your goals, make them specific and reachable. Vague or unattainable goals are the kind that frustrate. Who needs extra frustration? Pray through your goals. Ask the Lord to make his goals for you, your goals for you. Second Corinthians 5:9 says, "So we make it our goal to please him."

When we aim to please him, we find we're pleased right along with him. It's a key to joy. One that you won't have to hunt far to find.

> I have not yet reached my goal, and I am not perfect. But Christ has taken hold of me. So I keep on running and struggling to take hold of the prize. My friends, I don't feel that I have already arrived. But I forget what is behind, and I struggle for what is ahead. I run toward the goal, so that I can win the prize of being called to heaven. This is the prize that God offers because of what Christ Jesus has done. All of us who are mature should think in this same way. And if any of

you think differently, God will make it clear to you. But we must keep going in the direction that we are now headed.

Philippians 3:12–16 CEV

20 Purse on a Rope

We gals have to keep up with these handbags of ours wherever we go, don't we? Every once in a while I start feeling like I have another appendage. Since I've confessed to having so much trouble keeping up with my "extra appendage," I'll admit that I've thought about handcuffing myself to mine. Or maybe a nice rope would do it. I'm a Texas-born gal; I think I could hog-tie that rascal. Would a "yippee-yi-o-ki-yay" be appropriate here?

Even with all the attachment issues and despite all the trouble I have locating my bags, purses are still so ideal for carrying whatever we need to wherever we need to be that I can't see us ever amputating. How would we ever lug all our stuff from location A to location B without a purse? Maybe when we're looking for a new purse, instead of a salesperson we need a purse *realtor*. It's all about location, location, location.

I think, however, there's one location we've overlooked. I was all the way in the shower the other day before I remembered I didn't have my new shampoo in there. How many times have you been in the shower only to find you needed a new razor? Or your facial scrub? Or your favorite loofa?

What do we need? A shower purse! I got myself in an excited lather over the idea, but one of my friends said she thought it was all wet. I still say a "purse on a rope" would make a great shower accessory.

Maybe I could even make my own. A few measurements, the right-sized container, a glue-on rhinestone or two and I think I could put together one all-too-cute shower purse.

Measuring Up

I would have to be extra careful on the measuring part since numbers are not my best thing. Then again, sometimes even those math whizzes have trouble "measuring up." A few weeks ago, my college kids were home, and for some reason none of us can figure, Jordan decided to do some sort of ice cream circus act with our giant tub of ice cream. We have so many teenaged ice cream eaters that we buy the vat size. I'm not quite sure why the math and physics of it all didn't occur to Jordan, but he was joking around with his sister and started swinging the tub by its red handle in a straight-arm ferris-wheel kind of motion.

The calculations fell into place when the six-foot boy with the long arm span swung the giant ice cream tub underneath the kitchen light fixture. It crashed into the fixture, knocking the big glass dome cover off. The glass dome landed square on top of Jordan's head, knocking a nice knot on it. It was probably one of those "I coulda had a V8" math/physics moments. Then the dome fell to the floor and shattered into a gazillion glass slivers.

Poor Jordan. It took him forever to clean up all the glass. By the time he finished, the ice cream was almost melted—and he wasn't even sure he wanted any anymore.

Calculated Moves

I hate to tell you how many times I've caught myself in the same kind of stunt. Not with the big drum of ice cream. But I all too often catch myself forgetting my main life pursuit while being distracted by the temporary things of the world. Getting caught up in the world's way of thinking is a surefire way to guarantee a head-konking incident in my spiritual future. Those V8 moments are just a swing away.

First John 2:15–17 (CEV) says,

> Don't love the world or anything that belongs to the world. If you love the world, you cannot love the Father. Our foolish pride comes from this world, and so do our selfish desires and our desire to have everything we see. None of this comes from the Father. The world and the desires it causes are disappearing. But if we obey God, we will live forever.

Living in foolish pride and selfish desires? It's a life that's directionless and unfulfilled. It may even come with a knot on the head. But a life lived with a passionate consciousness of God and a deep desire to walk in holiness brings eternal fruit. It's the sweet life with fruit on top. Who needs ice cream?

Getting out of the pride and selfishness trap and staying true to our pursuit of holiness is as much about not fueling unholiness. It requires changing some habits. If you're watching or reading things that make unholiness look good and right and fun—even hilarious—it's time for a channel change. First Corinthians 6:18 says, "Run away from sexual sin!" (NLT[a]), and 2 Timothy 2:22 warns us to "flee the evil desires of youth, and pursue righteousness." Are you allowing yourself to stay in a situation where you know there is a temptation to think or act in an unholy direction? Your pride will tell you that you can handle it; but the best course of action is to *run*.

Make a Run for the Holy Life

Romans 13:12–14 (NKJV) says,

> The night is far spent, the day is at hand. Therefore let us cast off the works of darkness, and let us put on the armor of light. Let us walk properly, as in the day, not in revelry and drunkenness, not in lewdness and lust, not in strife and envy. But put on the Lord Jesus Christ, and make no provision for the flesh, to fulfill its lusts.

We need to make sure we're making no provision for the flesh. Anything that causes us to lose our thirst for righteousness, anything that hinders us in our pursuit—those are the things we must cast off. Is there a certain kind of book, magazine, website, TV program, movie, person, situation you need to flee? Are you willing to sacrifice it for the sake of holiness? Are you willing to run? Proverbs 27:12 says, "The prudent see danger and take refuge, but the simple keep going and suffer for it."

I have a friend who found herself thinking all the wrong thoughts each time she went in to see her chiropractor. It didn't help that she was struggling in her marriage at the time. But did she blame her husband that her mind was taking off in the wrong direction? Did she blame the doctor? Did she rationalize those wayward thoughts or try to reel them in on her own? No. She made no provision for the flesh. She ran. She found a new chiropractor. And she made herself accountable to a couple of her friends and asked us to keep a check on her in that matter. That's wisdom. And it's the kind of wisdom that can take us to new heights in the pursuit of holy living.

When was the last time you asked someone to pray for you in a specific area of your pursuit of holiness? When was the last time you made yourself accountable to someone in an area of temptation? It requires genuine humility—the type of humility that beautifully shows a person is pursuing holiness with all the zeal it's due.

First Peter 2:11 says, "Beloved, I beg you as sojourners and pilgrims, abstain from fleshly lusts which war against the soul" (NKJV).

No need to konk me over the head with a vat of ice cream. I get it. Avoiding the flesh wars is all part of pursuing a holy walk. Pursuing holiness involves a conscious decision to break the old habits and replace them with the habit of holiness. Out with that old way, in with the new.

"Train yourself to be godly" (NLT[b]) 1 Timothy 4:7 tells us. Forming habits of saying no to areas where we're vulnerable and saying yes to obedience and to holiness is exactly how we can make a clean start. You don't even need a purse on a rope for this kind of clean start.

And as long as we're making clean starts, after cleaning a gazillion shards of glass, I'm pretty sure Jordan has a new resolve not to try to wrangle his ice cream.

> Therefore do not let sin reign in your mortal body, that you should obey it in its lusts. And do not present your members as instruments of unrighteousness to sin, but present yourselves to God as being alive from the dead, and your members as instruments of righteousness to God. For sin shall not have dominion over you, for you are not under law but under grace.
>
> Romans 6:12–14 NKJV

Part 5

"But just as he who called you is holy"

21 Never Purse-nickety

It looks like a purse to me, but to at least one person in my household, it must look more like a drum than a handbag. My son Daniel is quite the musician. He's a fourteen-year-old guitar player, bass player, trombonist, and . . . have mercy . . . drummer. Daniel has a drum set, but I don't think it's really all that necessary. All of life is a drum to this boy. He was drumming on the top of the table the other day. My purse was on the floor, and it was (*stomp, stomp*) his bass drum. My purse—a purse-cussion instrument! By the end of his second drum solo, the granola bar I had in there was total granola dust.

Anything and everything is Daniel's drum. The sofa is his drum. The wall? Drum. The desk, the chair, his sister? Drum, drum, drum. He was baking cookies with me last week, and even the cookie sheet was a drum. Okay, actually that was more of a cymbal—but there was still definite drummage.

Daniel drums without even knowing he's drumming. It's the percussion that never ends. His auto-drum is on 24/7. The other day I couldn't stand it anymore. My left eye was twitching—on the beat. I said, "Daniel! Could you PLEASE stop percussing for five minutes?"

"Sure," he said without missing a beat (as it were). Then he looked at his watch.

He just beats all! I wish I had thought to say that to him that day. That's okay. I'm enjoying the drum-punnage right now enough for the both of us. All I need is a "pa-dum-*ching*."

Auto-routine

I wonder how many things I do without thinking. I'm not a big drummer, but no doubt there are a bazillion annoying auto-habits I'm not aware of that are causing eyes to twitch left and right.

The "as he who called you is holy" phrase of the 1 Peter passage we're focusing on in this section implies a couple of amazing truths: that he is holy, and that he called us. Those two truths affect everything we do. They affect how we see others and how we respond to them. We're called to respond to others in his love because he has made us his holy people. Colossians 3:12–14 (NCV[b]) spells it out:

> God has chosen you and made you his holy people. He loves you. So you should always clothe yourselves with mercy, kindness, humility, gentleness, and patience. Bear with each other, and forgive each other. If someone does wrong to you, forgive that person because the Lord forgave you. Even more than all this, clothe yourself in love. Love is what holds you all together in perfect unity.

The Love Beat Goes On

Oh, that my love for the Lord would cause me to grow to the place where there are more things I do without thinking that bless than things I do without thinking that annoy—more loving, less "purse-nickety." In 1 Corinthians 12:31, Paul says, "But now let me show you a way of life that is best of all" (NLT[b]). Then he begins what we call the "love chapter." Love should be a way of life for those of us who have been called out by a holy God. Loving others selflessly should happen as naturally and rhythmically as those *tap, tap, taps* on the desk—loving almost without having to think about it.

Verses 4–7 (NLT[b]) in 1 Corinthians 13 tell us what that kind of love looks like:

> Love is patient and kind. Love is not jealous or boastful or proud or rude. It does not demand its own way. It is not irritable, and it keeps no record of being wronged. It does not rejoice about injustice but rejoices whenever the truth wins out. Love never gives up, never loses faith, is always hopeful, and endures through every circumstance.

How important is our sacrificial love for others to our heavenly Father? We're told in 1 Corinthians 13:1 that we could speak every language on earth—we could even speak the language of angels. But if we don't love others, even Angel-ese sounds like a bunch of annoying noise. As a matter of fact, it says that without love, even if I'm speaking the sweetest language there is, "I would only be a noisy gong or a clanging cymbal" (NLT[b]). The last thing I want to do is cause a twitch in the eye of the God I love.

I want to love others because I am loved by and called by a holy God. And I want to love consistently, steadily—without missing a beat. Loving to beat the band—even at the kitchen table when my purse is the bass drum.

Cheese Drumming

I guess it's sort of related that I opened my microwave the other day and found another bass drum. This one was made of cheese. It was a big fat round mound of cheese cooked onto the bottom of the microwave. Someone obviously tried to make one of those nacho mountains. But how could you zap Mt. Nacho and not notice it's doing a volcano thing a couple of minutes in? And then how could you just walk away and leave all the cheese-lava smoldering there? Surely you'd at least notice something was up when you pulled the plate out, got halfway across the kitchen, then realized the plate was still connected to the microwave by a six-foot stretchy string of cheese. The orchestra is complete when you've got the percussion covered and you add the strings. Maybe it's inevitable when you have a houseful of teenagers who can ignore the drumming with their selective hearing and the lava with their selective vision.

It's about as easy to have selective vision in our spiritual lives sometimes too. Isn't it so much more pleasant to find a fault in someone else than it is to notice a weakness of our own? I don't even want to think about how many nacho-type messes I've noticed in others while stringing along a six-foot cheese-rope of my own.

But Jesus can give us a different kind of vision—vision that's not so quick to dismiss our own messes. In Matthew 7:3–5, he asks,

> Why do you look at the speck of sawdust in your brother's eye and pay no attention to the plank in your own eye? How can you say to your brother, 'Let me take the speck out of your eye,' when all the time there is a plank in your own eye? You hypocrite, first take the plank out of your own eye, and then you will see clearly to remove the speck from your brother's eye.

Jesus Vision

Jesus's kind of vision clears those hypocrisies right up. And his kind of vision is the kind that sees the best in others. His vision is filtered through love. It's never purse-nickety. First Corinthians 13:5 tells us that real love "is not rude, it is not self-seeking, it is not easily angered, it keeps no record of wrongs."

Loving according to the Lord's example and according to his calling will keep us on the right track and help us to consistently see things more clearly. It's not only better vision, it's the best vision. Even if you still completely miss the cheese ropes.

Let me add here that loving others doesn't mean we should embrace their worldly behavior. The Father's holy calling affects our choices in who we hang out with too. We can take the light of Jesus to those who live in darkness, but we don't need to live there in the dark. Our closest friends should be those who encourage us to live holy and those we can encourage in the holy walk right back.

Second Corinthians 6:14–18 in *The Message* says it this way:

> Don't become partners with those who reject God. How can you make a partnership out of right and wrong? That's not partnership; that's war. Is light best friends with dark? Does Christ go strolling with the Devil? Do trust and mistrust hold hands? Who would think of setting up pagan idols in God's holy Temple? But that is exactly what we are, each of us a temple in whom God lives. God himself put it this way:
>
> "I'll live in them, move into them;
> I'll be their God and they'll be my people.
> So leave the corruption and compromise;
> leave it for good," says God.
> "Don't link up with those who will pollute you.

> I want you all for myself.
> I'll be a Father to you;
> you'll be sons and daughters to me."

We are his children, called to holy living by a holy God. That calling affects every aspect of every relationship we have. O Lord, may we embrace our holy calling tighter and tighter in every relationship. Let your holiness influence who we relate to and how we relate to them. May we follow you every step of the way, and may we influence and love others in a way that will bless your name!

> Imitate God, therefore, in everything you do, because you are his dear children. Live a life filled with love, following the example of Christ. He loved us and offered himself as a sacrifice for us, a pleasing aroma to God. . . . Don't participate in the things these people do. For once you were full of darkness, but now you have light from the Lord. So live as people of light! For this light within you produces only what is good and right and true. Carefully determine what pleases the Lord. Take no part in the worthless deeds of evil and darkness; instead, expose them.
>
> Ephesians 5:1–2, 7–11 NLT[a]

---

22 Pick Yourself Up by Your Own Purse Straps

If you consistently carry one of the heavier-dutier purses like I do, you understand the danger of the shoulder callus. I've worried that I'm eventually going to look like the Hunchback of Notre Dame—even though I'm from St. Louie. I'm thinking of switching shoulders every few hours so I can build up calluses on both sides. Of course, then I'm in danger of looking less like a hunchback and more like a *linebacker* from Notre Dame.

Then again, one of the nice things about those shoulder calluses is that, after a while, you can't even feel the purse anymore. You can't feel anything at all anymore. Burlap purse strap? Bring it on. You could carry a rosebush on that numb shoulder.

High-Fiber Purse

I'm afraid to go burlap for one particular dog-related reason, however. Allie's puppy would probably look at a burlap purse strap and assume it was my attempt to provide her with the best high-fiber diet. I'm just sure it would look like Shredded Wheat to LuLu, the dog with the indiscriminate eating habits. Add milk and a little fruit and the entire purse could be part of her complete and balanced breakfast.

You wouldn't believe how many weird things that pup has eaten this week. I can hardly count. I can tell you that I fished a couple of triple A batteries from her little doggie molars just the other day. They must've charged her up because around lunchtime she had another one of her ink-pen cravings. I thought I had the pens all hidden, but she somehow found one. Before I caught her, LuLu had left two catastrophic blue ink spots on my carpet. One was about the size of a quarter, the other, a dime. Not that I'm used to interpreting ink spots or anything, but they looked very Dalmatian-like. And the big one was shaped remarkably like a profile of the Energizer Bunny—bass drum and everything. If a psychologist analyzed my interpretation, I wonder if he would tell me I have some deep-seated battery issues.

Assault and Batteries?

Ignoring the psychological battery implications, I decided to launch an assault on the stains. Time to get down to the battle of the ink blots. I gathered a large supply of skin-irritating chemicals and scrubbed until my hands throbbed and felt twice their original size. I stepped back to check my progress and found that the ink spots were twice their original size too. I had taken them from a quarter and a dime and combined them into one spot that equaled about forty-nine cents.

I gave it another ten minutes of elbow grease and then resurveyed. How could extra scrubbing add to the forty-nine cents? What, elbow grease *stains*? It looked like I had added at least three more quarters and a dime. Man! I was at a dollar thirty-four and climbing. I figured it was time to give up the rubbing and call in the professionals for some industrial-strength treatment.

Here's the Rub

Trying to make spiritual stains go away on our own is even more futile. When we try to work out our sin stains with our own elbow grease, we end up with an even bigger mess. We need to call in *the* Professional. The blood of Jesus is the one true stain remover. David said in Psalm 51:1–2 and 7,

> Have mercy on me, O God,
> according to your unfailing love;

according to your great compassion
 blot out my transgressions.
Wash away all my iniquity
 and cleanse me from my sin. . . .
Cleanse me with hyssop, and I will be clean;
 wash me, and I will be whiter than snow.

Just as a shoulder can get callused and unfeeling, our hearts can too. Sin is the rub. We sin once, we're bothered. We feel guilty, and we're truly disturbed that we have grieved the very Spirit of God. But when we continue to lug a sin around, and we allow it to rub away at our consciences, without confessing and forsaking it, our hearts can become hard and callused. If we truly want to pursue holy living, we can never allow ourselves to feel comfortable hauling around that burlap strap of sin.

First John 1:9 not only gives us our instruction in getting rid of the sin, but it's our promise of forgiveness and our encouragement to continue the pursuit of the life of holiness: "If we [freely] admit that we have sinned and confess our sins, He is faithful and just (true to His own nature and promises) and will forgive our sins [dismiss our lawlessness] and [continuously] cleanse us from all unrighteousness [everything not in conformity to His will in purpose, thought, and action]" (AMP).

Four-Way Confessing

Need a little four-step outline to help you know where to start? Try: (1) confessing frequently, (2) confessing fearlessly, (3) confessing fully, and (4) confessing freely.

1. Confess without fail—*frequently*. If living in personal holiness meant we would never sin again, then this phrase in its original

language would not include the inference that we have to keep it up—to keep on confessing. It's a perpetual part of the pursuit of holiness. God continues to forgive. We must consistently confess. "Confess" means to agree with. We need to agree with God that our sin is ugly and allow him to cleanse it; and we need to do it frequently, keeping a short distance between any sin and our confession.

2. Confess without apprehension—*fearlessly*. There's no need to fear. God hates sin, yes, but he loves you and he longs to see you making positive steps toward holiness. It's his desire to clean you up. Come to him without apprehension. Hebrews 4:15–16 tells us we can come to him bravely: "Jesus understands every weakness of ours, because he was tempted in every way that we are. But he did not sin! So whenever we are in need, we should come bravely before the throne of our merciful God. There we will be treated with undeserved kindness, and we will find help" (CEV).

3. Confess without holding back—*fully*. Name those sins. We commit our sins one by one. That's how we should confess them. It's not pretty and it's not fun, but it is necessary. When we offer a blanket "forgive my sins—Lord, you know what they are," we might not be as disturbed by the ugliness of our sins, but we need to be . . . well . . . *disturbed* about the ugliness of our sin. And we need to contemplate how completely disturbing our sin is to our holy God.

4. Confess without keeping the guilt—*freely*. Once we've confessed our sin, we need to accept the Father's forgiveness. We're free to move on, guilt-free. The price for that sin has been paid. Your just God will never ask you to keep paying for your sin when he's already paid the sin tab in full. His payment is eternally complete. Once you've confessed your sin,

pick yourself up (though not necessarily by your own purse straps) and move forward. Confess with the confidence that he has forgiven.

Andrew Murray explains so beautifully the significance of the confession of sin in our pursuit of holiness in *Deeper Christian Life*:

> Dear Christians, do you not long to be brought nigh unto God? Would you not give anything to walk in close fellowship with Jesus every day? Would you not count it a pearl of great price to have the light and love of God shining in you all the day? Oh, come and fall down and make confession of sin; . . . Bow very humbly, and cry very earnestly, "O God, reveal to me the carnal life in which I have been living: reveal to me what has been hindering me from having my life full of the Holy Ghost." Shall we not cry, "Lord, break my heart into utter self-despair, and, Oh! Bring me in helplessness to wait for the Divine power, for the power of the Holy Ghost, to take possession and to fill me with a new life given all to Jesus?"[1]

If an absence of consistent confession of sin has been keeping you from the holy life, will you let your heavenly Father forgive and restore you and get you back in the game where holiness is concerned? Get rid of any linebacker hardness and let Jesus make you clean and tender.

And if you're still building purse strap calluses, do be careful that no one mistakes you for a linebacker. Those surprise blitzes can be murder.

Those who live according to the sinful nature have their minds set on what that nature desires; but those who live in accordance with the Spirit have their minds set on what the Spirit desires. The mind of sinful man is death, but the mind controlled by the Spirit is life and peace; the sinful mind is hostile to God. It does not submit to God's law, nor can it do so. Those controlled by the sinful nature cannot please God.

You, however, are controlled not by the sinful nature but by the Spirit, if the Spirit of God lives in you. And if anyone does not have the Spirit of Christ, he does not belong to Christ. But if Christ is in you, your body is dead because of sin, yet your spirit is alive because of righteousness. And if the Spirit of him who raised Jesus from the dead is living in you, he who raised Christ from the dead will also give life to your mortal bodies through his Spirit, who lives in you.

Romans 8:5–11

23 The Purse Universe

Since my entire family is constantly tucking things into my purse when I'm not looking, I'm forever finding alien items in there. The good news is that I rarely mistake my purse for someone else's. Who else carries a Styrofoam model of planet Earth and a little matching Mercury? I've got the whole world in my purse—and then some.

On the not-so-good side, though, my purse really could start to develop its own ozone layer. What if foreign objects start to orbit? It could get so out of control that the thing could supernova. I'd hate to be carrying around my own tapestry-covered black hole. That's just too scary.

The Purse-ville Horror

We've never been one of those families that sits around a campfire telling scary stories. Those scary purse stories can be especially terrifying. Every once in a while, though, I have to admit I like to frighten my teenage girls with one of the scariest stories I know. And it happened to *me*. It's the story about when I was a little girl . . . and my mom (scary music building). . . . gave me . . . (insert a maniacal "mwah-ah-ah" here) . . . a HO-O-O-OME PER-ER-ER-ERM (now the shriek of terror)!

I describe in gory detail how I had to spend several weeks either wearing my purse on my head, or going purse-less and looking like a dandelion, the other cruel children making wishes and blowing on my head. Frightening, I tell you. Nothing can raise up a fresh batch of goose bumps like a story of evil monster-hair-forming chemicals and a perm gone bad.

What could be scarier than that first look in the mirror? You're pretty sure you're so frightened your hair is standing on end—but who could tell? After hearing my dandelion story, I think my girls would buy a home lobotomy kit before they would buy a home perm kit.

Didn't I hear this comment about that bottle of perm solution? "I'd rather have a frontal lobotomy than a bottle in front of me."

Spiritual Lobotomy Anyone?

How many people do you know who seem to have found a lobotomy blue-light special? How many ignore his holy call? Proverbs 9:10 says, "The fear of the Lord is the beginning of wisdom, and knowledge of the Holy One is understanding." Understanding our Holy God begins with a good kind of fear. Not the hair-curling kind of fear, but a humble, awed reverence for the holy, holy, holy God.

The more we know our holy God, and the more we understand his call to us and his call to service, the more we understand that he never calls us to do anything he doesn't equip us to do. He designed us. He packed our purse, as it were, with everything we need.

What if I did find a purse identical to mine (okay, it's a bit of a stretch to think we could find another bag with its own Earth and Mercury)? What would I do? Would I try to make do with someone else's purse goodies? Would I try to make her makeup work for me? Would I use her credit card? That could result in great frustration—and maybe jail time.

God has given you what you need to serve him. How many times do we shift our brains and spirits into neutral and ignore the gifts he's given us? We so often try to force someone else's bag to fit our needs.

Perfectly Packaged YOU!

Think about how your heavenly Father has designed, equipped, and packaged *you*. Part of the holy life is discovering how the Lord has wired you to serve, then obediently serving.

God never "packs a purse" by absentmindedly stuffing this gift in one pocket or cramming that talent in another one. No, with great care and unimaginable purpose he puts in exactly what we need to do what he's called us to do. Psalm 139:15–16 is a reminder: "My frame was not hidden from you when I was made in the secret place. When I was woven together in the depths of the earth, your eyes saw my unformed body. All the days ordained for me were written in your book before one of them came to be."

We are "woven together" like the most beautiful tapestry—no purse compares. Our loving Father chose the colors, each and every thread; he lovingly applied every ornamental piece of trim, every little sparkle. Your personality, your character, your gifts and talents—all those were clearly thought out and woven together before you were born. And for the highest, holiest purposes. Look at how the Amplified Version phrases that part of Psalm 139:15: "My frame was not hidden from You when I was being formed in secret [and] intricately and curiously wrought [as if embroidered with various colors]."

Your gift for organizing? It's from him. What are you doing with it? Your musical abilities? From him! How are you using them to bring him glory? Your math brain? He wired it. Are you crunching numbers to his honor?

You are handmade, not manufactured in mass. Every detail chosen with thought, deliberation, purpose. Fulfill that purpose. Be holy in everything you do, in every area you serve. First Peter 4:11 says, "If anyone ministers, let him do it as with the ability which God supplies" (NKJV). This is the place you'll find fulfillment, excitement about life, the adventure you're longing for—and a life that honors the holy God who designed you and called you.

Don't frustrate yourself by trying to serve in a way he hasn't called you or designed you to serve. If you're shuffling papers when he equipped you and purposed you to offer mercy and medicine to the sick, you'll find yourself burned out and fed up. And you'll find that pursuing holiness when you're frustrated and out of your element is exasperating like nothing else. Don't pursue work; pursue your holy calling. Don't pursue money; pursue your holy calling.

Purse-piration for Jesus

Whether it's your ministry or your job or the combo, understand that our time on Earth (the real one, not the purse-sized one) is short and precious. We can use it up going to work every day to make money. Or we can work every day to make a difference for Jesus and to fulfill our holy calling.

After Peter fished all night and caught nothing, Jesus told him to let out the nets one more time. What happened? More fish than they could handle. The nets were about to break, the boats about to sink. This was the ultimate catch. Bigger than Peter could even think. Bigger than his boat or his nets could hold. What made the difference in the frustrated, fruitless, fish-all-night-for-nothing toss of the net and the overflowing, up-to-their-waist-in-jumping-scales fish harvest? It was the presence of the holy Jesus.

Whether your boat is your cubicle or your kitchen, whether your purse sits in a locker at a factory or on a counter at home filled with pacifiers and burp towels, your work can be a place you honor Christ and grow in holiness. Why? Because you choose to let your work be all about his work. Colossians 3:17 says to "let every detail in your lives—words, actions, whatever—be done in the name of the Master, Jesus" (Message).

Even if your job is anything but uplifting and your boss is after you at every turn or the kids are challenging you at every step, take Jesus to work with you. His presence will make the difference. "Work with enthusiasm, as though you were working for the Lord rather than for people" (Ephesians 6:7 NLT[a]).

Do you want an easy life or a holy and satisfied one? Your work can be much less about fashioning your happiness and much more about fashioning your holiness.

As you see the Father fashioning your holiness, you might even find yourself surprised at how you're much less bothered about hair fashion tragedies. Whether your hair is curly, straight, or self-fried.

> For this reason I remind you to fan into flame the gift of God, which is in you through the laying on of my hands. For God did not give us a spirit of timidity, but a spirit of power, of love and of self-discipline. So do not be ashamed to testify about our Lord, or ashamed of me his prisoner. But join with me in suffering for the gospel, by the power of God, who has saved us and called us to a holy life—not because of anything we have done but because of his own purpose and grace. This grace was given us in Christ Jesus before the beginning of time, but it has now been revealed through the appearing of our Savior, Christ Jesus, who has destroyed death and has brought life and immortality to light through the gospel.
>
> 2 Timothy 1:6–10

---

24 It's a Landfill in a Bag

I have a dreadful tendency to let my purse go. Right now it's been entirely too long between cleanings. One of the worst parts of not giving the purse the attention it needs is that it's not as equipped for life as it usually is. I just noticed that my purse-sized Tylenol bottle is empty. My tin of mints is empty. Even my purse-sized lotion is running low—and I just can't let that happen. How can such a full purse be so empty?

Of course, the empty parts are still not quite as troublesome as some of the "fuller" parts—all those things growing out of hand. It's one thing for a purse not to be equipped for life. It's another for it to be growing its own life. I wonder if I can claim new microscopic life-forms as dependents on my tax return.

Not sure if your purse needs a good disinfecting? Here are some signs to watch for.

Top Ten Ways to Know You Need to Clean Your Purse

1. Every time you set it on the carpet, it leaves a stain
2. Someone puts a cigar out in it
3. It sets off Geiger counters
4. Everyone thinks it's a garage sale in a bag
5. The health department pastes a condemnation notice on it
6. So many strange things are growing on the outside of it that someone asks if it's a Chia-purse
7. Your friends won't sit downwind of you anymore
8. One of your kids asks if he can enter your purse in the school science fair
9. He wins
10. You have to call an exterminator . . . just for the purse . . . again

I may not always stay on top of purse sanitation issues, but I guarantee if I saw something swarming in there, I would call the exterminator guys in a heartbeat. They would likely sigh and say something like, "It's *her* again." That's because if I see even one bug anywhere in or near my house, those people get a call, no ifs, ands, or bugs. See, in my mind, one bug means we're infested. And while we're in my mind (not necessarily the safest place to be, by the way), I'll tell you that in there, all bugs are poisonous.

Deadly poisonous. And even if the bugs are having an off day and forget to poison you, they will still eat you.

Exterminator II—the Return of the Bug Guys

I can almost hear the exterminator people rolling their eyes every time I call. Can't you picture one of the guys covering the phone and telling his partner, "Guess what her 'deadly bug' is this week. It's a ladybug. Oh well, schedule us an easy hundred bucks for Tuesday."

Would you believe that even though the Father who called me is holy, holy, holy, he still never rolls his eyes when I call? It doesn't matter how often I've called or how many times he's had to convince me that I'm not going to be eaten, he responds to me according to his grace and in his love. What complete satisfaction there is there! It's satisfaction that never runs dry.

Since I mentioned my lotion bottle that's running intolerably low, let me tell you that even though I may have to clean all the unnecessary debris out of my purse when it starts to swarm, bugs or no bugs, I'll never get rid of my little purse bottle of lotion.

My husband has an entirely different lotion notion. He is convinced that lotion is scented slime imported from the place of the dead. Richie would sooner wallow in lard than use one of my creams. As a matter of fact, he says he can't understand how anyone can put that stuff on a clean body without feeling all dirty again.

He even goes so far as to make one of those pained-looking faces after I've driven his car post-lotion. He says it makes his steering wheel gooey. Picture him trying to drive using only a thumb and forefinger from each hand. Such a commotion over a little lotion!

But me? I love the stuff. To me, it's sort of medicinal and therapeutic all at the same time. I guess I'm a lotion lover because I'm one of those rather dry women (skin, not wit). If you're like me and can rub your hands together and make sparks, you know what I mean. When I put on a lotion potion, my hands make that *glub, glub, glub* sound.

I consider myself creamed to perfection when I'm so greasy my fingers keep sliding right off my laptop. If you're ever reading something I've written and you get to "dk7n>le#i4ig*20;slhc&mo$b," you don't need to worry. It's most likely a little lotion slip and you can picture me smiling—fully hydrated.

If I were Balm Queen, no one would ever be lotion-poor. Lotion for all! After I made sure no one was deprived of their lotions, I would go out and swim in my own personal pool of lotion. Of course, I'd never be able to get out. Just try climbing up a pool ladder when you've been swimming in lotion. That's okay. I'd be satisfied to soak in my own lotion ocean.

Never Runs Dry

Just as lotion satisfies a dry woman, the same God who answers without an eye roll when we call will satisfy our thirsty souls. What an amazing privilege it is to be able to call on the God who hydrates us at the very center of who we are. Psalm 63:1–3 says,

> God, You are my God; I eagerly seek You.
> I thirst for You;
> my body faints for You
> in a land that is dry, desolate, and without water.
> So I gaze on You in the sanctuary
> to see Your strength and Your glory.

My lips will glorify You
because Your faithful love is better than life.

HCSB

The holy God who called us is the God who quenches. When we seek him and desire him in this dry place, he satisfies oh so much more than the best lotions and creams. He fills our every real need by his strength and for his glory. And it's all out of his faithful love for us. Better than lotion. Better than life!

A soul-thirsty woman encountered Jesus at a well. He said to her, "Everyone who drinks this water will be thirsty again, but whoever drinks the water I give him will never thirst. Indeed, the water I give him will become in him a spring of water welling up to eternal life" (John 4:13–14).

The holy life is a satisfied life. I love sharing the message of the satisfied life with others. I love passing it on to my children. There's nothing more thrilling as a parent than seeing their young thirsts quenched!

On the lotion front, however, my kids haven't exactly picked up my mind-set. That's okay. I'd much rather they get a hand in eternal satisfaction than a hand in the lotion-related kind. But I still thought they would love it when I bought those tissues with lotion added right in. I asked Andrew how he liked them. He said to direct all other such questions to his attorney. There's a lot of his father in that boy.

Oh give thanks to the Lord, for He is good;
For His lovingkindness is everlasting.
Let the redeemed of the Lord say so,
Whom He has redeemed from the hand of the adversary,
And gathered from the lands,
From the east and from the west,

From the north and from the south.
They wandered in the wilderness in a desert region;
They did not find a way to an inhabited city.
They were hungry and thirsty;
Their soul fainted within them.
Then they cried out to the LORD in their trouble;
He delivered them out of their distresses.
He led them also by a straight way,
To go to an inhabited city.
Let them give thanks to the LORD for His lovingkindness,
And for His wonders to the sons of men!
For He has satisfied the thirsty soul,
And the hungry soul He has filled with what is good.

Psalm 107:1–9 NASB

25

Purse-severe!

My purse has a yummy chocolaty center. Right now I have a handful of kisses in there, a half a bag of Peanut M&M's that I've had to put back in the bag from the bottom of my purse a couple of times (they're a little fuzzy but still good), a packet of instant hot cocoa, and a Snickers that was liquid at one point but has returned again to a solid state. In my thinking, though one of those purse-sized Whitman's Samplers certainly wouldn't hurt, that's still a fairly well-chocolate-stocked handbag. I may pick up the sampler later today. I don't ever want to be thought of as a chocolate slacker. I heard someone once say, "I'd stop eating chocolate, but I'm no quitter."

I'm persevering in hauling around the chocolate-centered purse. It's not so much about carrying around a little treat now and then. No, it's more about survival.

Choco-survival

Some may think I'm exaggerating when I say that chocolate is a matter of life and death. And I know you've already been clued in to the fact that math isn't my best thing, but if you'll crunch a few numbers with me (and maybe a few Peanut M&M's) I think you'll see my chocolate point.

Here's how it works for me. My favorite hunk o' chocolate has 150 calories. For me, chocolate is medicinal, so I take it in its personally prescribed dosage: "Take one chunk three times daily; increase prescribed amount as needed."

At three servings a day, we're talking about just over 164,000 calories a year. Since 3500 calories is measured in about one pound of body weight, that's about 47 pounds a year. I've been consistently taking my daily doses of chocolate for at least the past 15 years. Without my medicinal chocolate and its 47 added yearly pounds, I would be missing over 700 pounds of my present body weight. Since I weigh about 125, that means I would weigh *negative* 575 pounds. I would've ceased to exist about five years ago!

There it is. Mathematical proof that I need my chocolate-centered purse to survive.

Seriously though, as necessary as chocolate is for my physical "health," I really and truly do need to make sure I don't wimp out in the matter of holy living. Perseverance is as wrapped up in spiritual health as a Hershey bar is wrapped in foil. Paul gives us some clues in how to persevere in holiness in Philippians 1:10: "For I want you to understand what really matters, so that you may live pure and blameless lives until Christ returns" (NLT[b]). The more we understand what really matters, the more we're able to walk in holiness—in a pure and blameless life. And what is it that really matters? Knowledge of him!

More, More, More!

It bears repeating. Know him more, know holiness more. The pursuit of holiness shouldn't be the result of simply wanting to be a good person so we can feel better about ourselves. It's a calling. His calling. If we're essentially calling ourselves, it's not truly a call to holiness; it's a call to self-righteousness. That's a Pharisee-kind of holiness. Look at what Jesus said to them in Matthew 23:25–28:

> Woe to you, teachers of the law and Pharisees, you hypocrites! You clean the outside of the cup and dish, but inside they are full of greed and self-indulgence. Blind Pharisee! First clean the inside of the cup and dish, and then the outside also will be clean. Woe to you, teachers of the law and Pharisees, you hypocrites! You are like whitewashed tombs, which look beautiful on the outside but on the inside are full of dead men's bones and everything unclean. In the same way, on the outside you appear to people as righteous but on the inside you are full of hypocrisy and wickedness.

Nasty, isn't it? It's about as opposite a yummy chocolate center as you can get. Dirty dishes and dead men's bones. And that's only a little sample of the self-righteous "woes" Jesus gave the Pharisees (nothing whatsoever like the Whitman's kind of Sampler).

Holiness is not just a list of dos and don'ts. The Pharisees had long lists like that, and Jesus told us plainly that their kind of "righteousness" is not pretty. It's not about legalistic self-righteousness. It's about knowing him more and it's about the borrowed righteousness of Christ. It's knowing him and depending on his Holy Spirit for growing in holiness and going higher in our walk with Christ.

Philippians 3:10 says, "[My determined purpose is] that I may know Him [that I may progressively become more deeply and intimately acquainted with Him, perceiving and recognizing and understanding the wonders of His person]" (AMP).

In the fourth chapter we looked at 2 Peter 1:3, which tells us that "his divine power has given us everything we need for life and godliness through our knowledge of him who called us by his own glory and goodness." Everything we need for the holy life is wrapped up in the knowledge of him. And the last part of that verse is a reminder to us that our call to holiness is not about us. It's "by his own glory and goodness." Though there is great blessing in the holy life, the pursuit should never be about what's in it for *me*. It's about his glory.

Let's PURSE-sist!

Holiness is not just for your pastor or for the leaders of your women's ministry. It's not just for the guys on TV or your Sunday School teacher. It's for you. He calls each of us to holy living. Let's not be quitters!

That passage we looked at in Philippians 1:10 tells us that we are to live holy until Christ's return. What a day that will be! And we have a wonderful future promised to us if we've given our hearts and lives to Christ. It's a better-than-chocolate-three-times-a-day future and a glorious life empowered by the God of all power.

As for my physical future, I guess I'd better make sure I keep getting my daily doses of chocolate. After all, I could be a mere 2.65957 years from extinction.

> I pray that your hearts will be flooded with light so that you can understand the wonderful future he has promised to those he called. I want you to realize what a rich and glorious inheritance he has given to his people. I pray that you will begin to understand the incredible greatness of his power for us who believe him. This is the same mighty power that raised Christ from the dead and seated him in the place of honor at God's right hand in the heavenly realms. Now he is far above any ruler or authority or power or leader or anything else in this world or in the world to come.
>
> Ephesians 1:18–21 NLT[a]

Part 6

"So be holy in all you do"

26 The Bottomless Purse

Mary Poppins—now there's a gal who knew how to pack a purse. She could pull the Seven Wonders of the World out of that bottomless bag. A coat rack, a mirror—do I remember seeing a roast beef in there?

Mary pulled out a *potted plant*, no less. Not exactly on the short list of "a few of my favorite things," but I will say it's definitely on the unusual side. I haven't seen a lot of houseplants popping out of handbags, though you already know that it's not that unusual for me personally to pull something vegetation-related out of my purse. Having items that are alive and growing inside a handbag is not the unusual part. The especially unusual part is that the plant life that came out of the Poppins' bag was something that was actually nice to share. Nothing that's alive and growing that has come out of my purse has ever been anything I would actually relish sharing—or anything anyone else would relish receiving either. Certainly nothing decorative. The Poppins plant was not only ornamental, but it was one that wouldn't be considered a health hazard to boot. Impressive.

Pulling a fully grown plant out of a handbag would be one giant step beyond MiracleGro. I think if I had a Mary Poppins-type carpet bag, I would consider opening a greenhouse business. All those instant plants could be a landscaping goldmine.

Personally, I enjoy living in the age of instants. For instance (or "for instants"), I like my instant potatoes, instant soup, instant oatmeal—even Instant Messaging. I'm quite sure someone will eventually come up with instant H_2O—just add water.

Instant Holiness

So how about instant holiness? Wouldn't it be great if we could move closer toward the life of holiness by using the instant kind of holiness? A "just add water" kind of holiness! Or maybe a twelve-step program would make it easier. How about a pill your doctor could prescribe? "Take 1 holiness capsule 3 times daily for 14 days. No refills needed." Perfect holiness would be just a couple of weeks away.

But there is no Mary Poppins carpet bag with magic holiness tucked inside. There's no such thing as any of those easy routes to holiness. And while we've already looked at the passage in which God told us the holy life is not too hard for us to accomplish, that doesn't mean we'll never have to work at it.

Everything in our flesh screams for us to take the path of least resistance. That's the worldly path, and we'll never find holiness there. Hebrews 12:14 says, "*Make every effort* to live in peace with all men *and to be holy;* without holiness no one will see the Lord" (emphases mine).

Just as living at peace with those around us sometimes takes some work, so does living in holiness. "Make every effort" doesn't sound like the instant, easy road to me. Effort might even require a little muscle. The New Living Testament (NLT[b]) phrases 2 Corinthians 7:1 this way: "Let us work toward complete holiness."

We need to dwell on it, sacrifice for it, *work* toward it. Trading that easy road for the road to holiness is a trade we'll never regret.

Still, I'll admit I've looked for an extra clause in the phrase "so be holy in all you do" that's the focus of this section. Wouldn't "so be holy in most of the things you do" be a lot less daunting? "Be holy every time you feel like it" would work into our agenda a lot more easily too. But I couldn't find either of those little provisos. It seems to me it's a bigger job than pulling a full-sized potted plant out of my average-sized handbag.

A big job requires a big God. It's the kind of job that only can happen as the result of an inner working of God's Holy Spirit. That doesn't mean, however, that our part is always going to be a cinch. It doesn't mean that it will require no discipline, no effort, no *work* on our part. We need to be willing to invest in holiness—to work at it. Are you willing to exert effort toward holiness, even when it's tough?

Holy Action

Take a look at 2 Corinthians 7:1 in the New King James Version: "Therefore, having these promises, beloved, let us cleanse ourselves from all filthiness of the flesh and spirit, perfecting holiness in the fear of God." "Perfecting" in this context is a verb, an action word. And perfecting holiness will always require action. Our holiness should be alive and growing—in the biggest, best way.

Praise the God who not only gives us the muscle to work hard but infuses us with the "want to" as well. Philippians 2:12–13 says, "Work hard to show the results of your salvation, obeying God with deep reverence and fear. For God is working in you, giving you the desire and the power to do what pleases him"

(NLT[b]). The desire and the power—he's working them both in us. We can find ourselves oh so pleasantly surprised at what our God is able to pull out of us. We're like the Poppins bag to the max! Who would've thought we could be so tickled to be bag ladies?

> Work out (cultivate, carry out to the goal, and fully complete) your own salvation with reverence and awe and trembling (self-distrust, with serious caution, tenderness of conscience, watchfulness against temptation, timidly shrinking from whatever might offend God and discredit the name of Christ). Not in your own strength for it is God Who is all the while effectually at work in you, energizing and creating in you the power and desire, both to will and to work for His good pleasure and satisfaction and delight. Do all things without grumbling and faultfinding and complaining against God and questioning and doubting among yourselves, that you may show yourselves to be blameless and guiltless, innocent and uncontaminated, children of God without blemish (faultless, unrebukable) in the midst of a crooked and wicked generation, spiritually perverted and perverse, among whom you are seen as bright lights (stars or beacons shining out clearly) in the dark world, holding out to it and offering to all men the Word of Life.
>
> Philippians 2:12–16 AMP

---

27 Purse Your Lips

Lips make their own fashion statement, don't they? That's why a well-stocked purse can play a big role in first-rate lip style. Everything lip-chic is tucked into the lip-care-conscious handbag.

For example, lipsticks in shades of red, pink, burgundy, and coral are basic essentials. Not one. One of each. Since lips should never clash with the clothing, we need to have every outfit hue possibility covered. And for some reason that I don't think anyone really understands, all those colors are required to have names that make you feel a little silly. Luscious Lily Mango, Passion Perky Pink, Eastern Desert Rose, Vixen Tart Wine, Mysteriously Misty Mauve, Luminous Caviar Blush, Glazed Vicious Frost—those are the ones you apply quickly while trying to hide the label. As a pastor's wife, I just can't afford to get caught rubbing "Vixen Tart Wine" on my lips—even if it is the only shade that complements my purple suit.

Then there are the glosses. If you have enough of the right kind, you can put a shine on those lips that friends can see themselves in. Personally, I like those luminously shimmering glosses—the kind that are just this side of an eye injury. I think they should name my favorite "Minor Retinal Damage."

A correctly stocked bag also includes ointments and creams in tubes, little jars, and sticks that can moisturize and heal lips from here to the Sahara. These are the lip balms that could turn a raisin back into a grape. An appropriately lip-stocked purse is a miracle balm in a bag.

Sealed with a What?

While we all want a purse that's equipped and ready to meet any lip need, let me mention that you do need to take care not to put the wrong thing on your lips. I had a friend who reached for her Chapstick and accidentally grabbed her glue stick instead. I don't want to embarrass her, so I can't tell much about it; my lips are sealed. But for the record, so were hers. It puts a whole new spin on SWAK, doesn't it? Surely that's not the right way to purse your lips.

No matter what I mistakenly put on my lips, I seriously doubt I would ever accidentally try a hot coal. Sealed with a hot coal? Ouch. But believe it or not, that's exactly what happened to Isaiah. In the sixth chapter of Isaiah we're told about Isaiah's encounter with the holy God. He saw him sitting on a throne in all his holiness, angels surrounding him and praising him, saying, "Holy, holy, holy is the Lord Almighty; the whole earth is full of his glory" (v. 3). The whole place shook with their praises and the temple was filled with smoke.

When was the last time you spent time dwelling on the holy, holy, holiness of our God? May I encourage you not to neglect experiencing the awe his holiness rightly inspires? He isn't merely holy. Not merely holy, holy. He is holy, holy, holy! There is no one holier.

Slip of the Lip

As we spend time contemplating his holiness and worshiping him, it never fails that we are suddenly painfully aware of our own unholiness. That's what happened to Isaiah too. After encountering God's holiness, he cries, "Woe to me! . . . I am ruined! For I am a man of unclean lips, and I live among a people of unclean lips, and my eyes have seen the King, the Lord Almighty" (Isaiah 6:5).

The lips represented the life. There was no lip balm of any color or consistency in any purse on earth that could accomplish an adequate lip repair for Isaiah. He knew he was a sinful man who lived with sinful people in the presence of a holy God.

As I started writing this book, I knew it was an opportunity for me. Not simply an opportunity to have a purseload of fun, but an opportunity to go on a holiness-seeking mission. I've prayed through the entire process and long before it began (and no doubt, will continue to pray long after the last chapter is finished). That prayer has been: "Lord, give me new glimpses into your holiness. And make me holy, because you are holy."

It shouldn't have surprised me that as he has given me new glimpses into his holiness, I've had bigger, ugly glimpses of my own sinfulness of the most Isaiah-esque kind. A look at his holy, perfect love, and I'm suddenly aware of how wimpy my own ability to love is and how selfish I can be. He's shown me how often I get wrapped up in what others think of me instead of what he thinks of me. And more. It hasn't been pretty. And it certainly hasn't been painless.

In verses 6 and 7 we're told that one of the seraphs took a live coal from the altar with tongs, flew to Isaiah, touched it to his lips, and said, "See, this has touched your lips; your guilt is taken away and your sin atoned for."

How can we ever sufficiently thank the God who has cleansed our lips, our lives, by the sacrifice of Jesus on the cross? Jesus is our burning coal. When we become aware of his awesome holiness and painfully aware of our own unholiness, let it drive us to our knees in thanks and praise and worship of the One who touched his own holiness to our lips in the lip balm of all lip balms. So much more than a lip balm—a life balm. And let it propel us into service. That's exactly what happened to Isaiah. Verse 8 says, "Then I heard the voice of the Lord saying, 'Whom shall I send? And who will go for us?'" Isaiah had just seen the holiness of God, and his own unholiness has been cleansed. He was in awe of God, thankful for his grace and cleaned up and ready to serve. He answered, "Here am I. Send me!"

Lip Service

Seeing God's holiness and experiencing his forgiveness completely transforms your life. It transforms the very heart of who you are. It's a transformation that translates into "Lord, send me!" as the sincere cry of our lips.

There is no true pursuit of holiness without understanding the ugliness of sin, and there is no true pursuit of holiness without allowing the Holy Spirit to cleanse us and to transform our way of thinking, our way of living—our way of serving.

Let me confess one more time my absolute unworthiness to write a book that includes the topic of holiness. I also confess that it would've been so much easier to let the deep theologians write the holiness book. Shouldn't I just stick to the chick laughs? Yet the importance of women seeking to live in holiness wouldn't let me merely skim over it. Pursuing holiness is the difference between living a life that makes a difference and an existence with nothing eternally worthwhile. It's the difference between a joyful, fulfilled life and a shallow, frustrated one.

Sadly, not all that many people are interested in holiness. This book would likely look much better on the store shelves if we tweaked the title to *Purse-suit of Happiness*. Can we agree together to let our pursuit be about holiness? It's not even about where the Lord chooses to send us. Frankly, Isaiah didn't get an easy job.

It's not about the job he gives us. It's not about the results. The message Isaiah had to deliver was not one that was well received. His sending involved delivering a message of judgment. But our sending is not a contract with conditions. God is the sender. We simply go. That's walking in obedience—that's living in holiness.

Holy living is what it's all about—whether you're bare-lipped or wearing Radical Ruby Red fortified with vitamin E.

In the year that King Uzziah died, I saw the Lord seated on a throne, high and exalted, and the train of his robe filled the temple. Above him were seraphs, each with six wings: With two wings they covered their faces, with two they covered their feet, and with two they were flying. And they were calling to one another:

"Holy, holy, holy is the LORD Almighty;
the whole earth is full of his glory."

At the sound of their voices the doorposts and thresholds shook and the temple was filled with smoke. "Woe to me!" I cried. "I am ruined! For I am a man of unclean lips, and I live among a people of unclean lips, and my eyes have seen the King, the LORD Almighty." Then one of the seraphs flew to me with a live coal in his hand, which he had taken with tongs from the altar. With it he touched my mouth and said, "See, this has touched your lips; your guilt is taken away and your sin atoned for." Then I heard the voice of the Lord saying, "Whom shall I send? And who will go for us?" And I said, "Here am I. Send me!"

Isaiah 6:1–8

---

28 Get Some Purse-pective

Having trouble keeping up with all the latest purse styles? Feeling your pain. But then again, high fashion is in the eye of the beholder, isn't it? Sometimes it's all in how you look at it. We just need a little purse-pective!

Maybe you have a bag that's out-of-date enough to drag your overall chic-factor down and you simply don't know it. Need a little help in ID-ing those out of style handbags? Here's a handful of signs of telltale, "style is stale" purse fashion failure.

Top Ten Ways You Can Tell Your Purse Is Out of Style

1. It was considered "last season" more than ten seasons ago
2. The purse is older than any piece of clothing in your closet
3. The purse is older than you
4. You're watching reruns of *Andy Griffith* and you notice Aunt Bea has the very same handbag
5. Someone tells you it's "totally groovy"—or worse, it's "the cat's meow"
6. It has a matching snood
7. The National Purse Historical Society labels it Vintage Colonial
8. You find out it was once used as a saddlebag for the Pony Express
9. It has a tag that reads "Made in Gomorrah"
10. You've been told it was a real find—an *archaeological* find

I've carried my share of dino-purses that some might consider an archaeological discovery. Or maybe it would be paleontological. As a matter of fact, I think the lining on the purse I'm using right now is starting to fossilize a little. The good news is that everyone likes it better since I turned it inside out. It seems the fossil look is all the rage. Who knew?

Jurassic Purse

No bones about it. Whether you're carrying a Gucci or a T-Rexxie, the trends will still come and go. On a side note, if you got your Gucci bag off the back of a truck from a guy named Shifty Larry, there's a chance you didn't get the dog of a deal you thought you did. Your Gucci might be more of a poochie. My advice when that happens? Just turn the bag inside-out. Couldn't hurt.

In a sort of connected incident, our pooch was supposed to stay inside but made one of those slick maneuvers out the front door the other day. I tried screaming doggie cookie bribes, but she saw a car and flew after it. Why do dogs do that? Does chasing a car make any sense whatsoever? What was she going to do if she caught it? She's half the size of one hubcap. Did she think she was going to wrestle the car to the ground and show it who's boss?

I would mock her a little more, but I can actually be much too much like that to get away with it for very long. My thinking can get oh so inside out—and not in a stylish way. It's like I decide I'm going to chase down living a holy life myself. Yeah, watch me; I can wrestle down that car!

But living a righteous life comes from giving God's Holy Spirit control—not from taking control myself. It's an inside job that affects the outside life. Now that's stylin'. As I give him control, he makes a holy life possible. And that's where I need to stay. Yes, I think the pup and I both need to learn to "sit" and "stay." Our Father works the learning into our lives by his Holy Spirit.

Inside Joke

How amazing it is that the Lord is willing to work on our insides. I thought about it again the other day when I was having breakfast with my kids. As we were all talking and laughing, one of my college boys said something out of the blue like, "Yeah, and then the rats would put on their jammies." Something like that, I don't remember exactly, because it made absolutely no sense whatsoever. He was laughing uproariously at whatever rat joke he had just told. The rest of us were just sitting there, smiling and blinking . . . and processing . . . waiting for his joke to make sense. But we totally didn't get it.

Kaley finally broke the silence with, "Jordan. You just told an inside joke where *you* were the only one *inside*, didn't you!" Jordan gave a half grin and said, "Yeah, but if my roommate had been here, he would've been laughing really hard." Then we *all* laughed really hard at the fact that Jordan was having such fun with his roommate—even though his roommate wasn't here!

Know what? It's even more fun with Jesus. He's always on the inside—even if we don't see him. He's always in on it. And that's a good thing. Even those times when we totally don't get it—we don't understand exactly how he's working in a situation—we can rest in knowing that he really is here, and he's working not only on the situation but on *us*—on the inside.

And isn't it beautiful how the inside affects the outside? Maybe we're more stylish, too, when we're inside out! We looked at Philippians 2:13 as a wonderful reminder that "it is God who works in you to will and to act according to his good purpose." And in Romans 8:28 we're told that he can do that work through absolutely any situation: "And we know that in all things God works for the good of those who love him, who have been called according to his purpose." It's better than an inside joke (though those are so fun). It's an inside *work*. And when the work is finished, we look more like Jesus than we did before.

Inside Up

God's way is so often opposite the world's way. Inside out, even. But as we control the outside influences, and as we remember the Holy Spirit's inside influence, we can see things more clearly from the Father's perspective. That's how we can keep our inside thoughts going in God's most "up" direction.

We've talked about our thoughts and our minds. Those thoughts come with the cost of consequences. Proverbs 23:7 makes it clear:

"For as he thinks within himself, so he is" (NASB). If we allow our sinful flesh to control our thoughts, or if we carelessly invite the Enemy into our way of thinking, those thoughts will show up in our actions.

But 2 Corinthians 10:4–5 says, "We fight with weapons that are different from those the world uses. Our weapons have power from God that can destroy the enemy's strong places. We destroy people's arguments and every proud thing that raises itself against the knowledge of God. We capture every thought and make it give up and obey Christ" (NCV[b]).

Capturing every thought and retraining the mind is not only a physical possibility, but it's a spiritual necessity for holy living. Capturing those rogue thoughts is part of the battle—and we know the mind is a battlefield. That's why we must set our minds on Christ and then guard that setting. It's like placing a soldier at the entrance of our minds, giving him the orders to guard that entrance. Remember, our minds are the control centers of our lives. Give up control to anything or anyone other than the Father? That's upside-down living in all the wrong ways. We need to keep that Holy Spirit Guard over our minds and keep Jesus at the center of our thoughts.

Inside Information

That's the kind of inside information we can really use. Giving the Holy Spirit complete control and allowing him to guard our thinking is the best way to keep the inside and the outside holy. And it doesn't matter in the least whether our purses are inside out, upside down, or made of the most genuine-looking faux fossil.

By the way, if I'm carrying an ancient Roman purse and my friends make fun of me, does that mean I'm being *purse-secuted*?

God himself put it this way:

"I'll live in them, move into them;
I'll be their God and they'll be my people.
So leave the corruption and compromise;
leave it for good," says God.
"Don't link up with those who will pollute you.
I want you all for myself.
I'll be a Father to you;
you'll be sons and daughters to me."
The Word of the Master, God.

With promises like this to pull us on, dear friends, let's make a clean break with everything that defiles or distracts us, both within and without. Let's make our entire lives fit and holy temples for the worship of God.

2 Corinthians 6:18–7:1 Message

29 Dis-purse-ing the Joy

Have you ever had to carry around a purse with a busted buckle, snap, or zipper? With a purse latch that won't catch well, you can easily end up accidentally disbursing all the contents of your purse all along the way, everywhere you go. Or would that be dis-*purse*-ing?

If you're like me, any buckle or snap problem is usually the result of overstuffing the purse within an inch of its zippered life—and beyond. It's like trying to stuff a couple of pounds of beef into one little enchilada. Leave it to me to want a cute, tiny purse that will still hold enough stuff to satisfy my every whim—without any kind of meat-plosion. I'm telling you, I want the whole enchilada.

When my purse gets overstuffed and I end up carrying my driver's license in my shoe because I just can't squeeze it in, I'm generally tempted to give up on the bulging zipper and borrow a couple of those hooked bungee cords from my husband's toolbox. I think the only reason I don't follow through on the bungee is that I'm such an over-stuffer, I think I could snap one. One bungee-twang in the wrong direction and that thing could rocket into the next neighborhood. I'd hate to hit a neighbor—even one who's not on my street. And what if I accidentally popped the bungee in my own direction? That would leave a mark for sure. I'm not one to live on the edge like that.

What's the Catch?

If I'm going to get a thrill from living on the edge, I think I'd like it to be mall-related instead of a purse-catch threat. Personally, I get a real charge from a lengthy shopping trip (ooh, did I say "charge"?). My husband would rather risk a severe pop from a runaway bungee. He has told me more than once that he would rather smash his thumb with a hammer than have to make a trip to the mall.

On the other hand, Richie loves a long bike trip on a nature trail. Totally not my idea of a good time. Heat, bugs, poison ivy, and straining muscles I don't even have? Just go ahead and pass me the hammer. And a large dose of a strong pain reliever.

Thrills, chills, and pain pills may vary from person to person and from hammer to hammer, but there is only one who should thrill us to our very soul. Only Jesus should be the absolute thrill of our lives. I love the hymn that includes the words:

> All that thrills my soul is Jesus
> He is more than life to me[1]

Thrilled to the Soul

Several times a day I have to ask myself if he really is more than life to me. From the grandest sale at the mall to the scenic nature trail, he is the maker, the reason for it all—he is all of life. No, even more. He's *more* than life.

How easily life can become more to me than my Savior. I can too often be such a spiritual wimp at even the slightest distraction. Colossians 1:17 reminds me that he is more than life—whether I recognize it or not. "And He is before all things, and in Him all things consist" (NKJV). He is the holy one who *is* life. And he is the only one who can direct us to live our lives in the way of holiness: "It is God who directs the lives of his creatures; everyone's life is in his power" (Job 12:10 GNT).

Know what's funny? Life in his power is the only place to find real thrills. Never think the instruction "so be holy in all you do" is a life sentence to tedium. No boredom here! The holy life is a life of thrills—it's a life of great joy! Maybe someday I'll write my own hymn about it. It could go something like this:

> He is my trip to the mall for the biggest sale
> He is my husband's bike ride on a long nature trail
> He is the most magnificent deep soul-thriller
> And so much better than any goofy pain-killer.

The joy-life of holiness is not about having everything fall into place just so-so. It doesn't mean there are never any bungee snaps. But it's a life of living without the burden unholiness brings. Hebrews 1:9 repeats Psalm 45:7 when it says, "You have loved righteousness and hated wickedness; therefore God, your God, has set you above your companions by anointing you with the oil of joy." Dis-purse the joy!

Let's find our every thrill and our very life in the power of the Savior. There is such joy in the sweet fellowship we experience when we're in his presence—and we can only find ourselves living in the sweet fellowship of his presence as we're walking in holiness.

Joy Dis-purse-ers

One of the best things about joy is that it spreads. Do you have people in your life who tickle your soul? Are there friends in your circle who make you think of the joy of Jesus every time you're with them? Those joyful friends are real people-magnets, aren't they? Don't you love to be around a joyful person?

Are you that kind of person to others? Are people encouraged to be more joyful just because they've been with you?

Did you know that you have a lot to say about how much of the joy of Christ you experience? Not because he gives you less or someone else more. But because you opt in every situation whether or not to grab hold of it. You get to choose. Through the presence of Christ, joy is ever available to you. Will you choose to live in it?

Joy in the life of holiness is like flying a flag of delight, letting those around you know that Jesus makes a difference in your life. The joy you can have because you know him is unshakable, unchanging, and eternal.

When my children were little, we regularly sang with great fervor the song that says, "Joy is the flag flown high from the castle of my heart . . . that says the King is in residence here"[2] Joy-filled believers are the beautiful "flags" that convince others that Jesus changes lives—from the heart/castle, out.

Castle, Sweet Castle

It's thrilling that the castle of my heart is secure. But every once in a while, my earthly castle starts to look like someone busted the latch on it too. It's like a leaky purse with stuff flowing everywhere. The past couple of weeks have been the impossibly busy kind, and there's been no time to catch up on my castle-work. Of course, when something has to go from my to-do list, I have to admit, I really love scratching the house-cleaning off the list.

Imagine me trying to be sincere as I whine, "I so wish I had time for that dusting, but, alas, I just can't squeeze it in today."

But now it's getting a little out of control. If it's true that a messy home is a happy home, we're nearing hysterics here. So I've decided to revisit the plan where we just leave the dust where it is, put a nice urn on the coffee table, and if anyone drops by unexpectedly, we simply say, "Yeah, I know it's a little different, but this is where Great Aunt Hepsebeth asked us to spread her ashes."

Okay, I admit it. There are better things we can spread. Joy for instance. We can spread the joy of the holy life to others. Disbursing joy! Psalm 9:11 says, "Tell his stories to everyone you meet" (Message). Whether we meet them at the grocery store, on the job, at school, at the gym—we can even spread the joyful news of our God who saves to those who come to our door unexpectedly.

There's an entire cropful of people who need to hear. What a high and holy privilege it is to disburse the good news of joy to them. The joyless people are everywhere we look—practically sitting in their own ashes. And every time we tell his stories, we're planting seeds. Jesus said in John 4:35–36, "Look around you! Vast fields are ripening all around us and are ready now for the harvest. The harvesters are paid good wages, and the fruit they harvest is people brought to eternal life. What joy awaits both the planter and the harvester alike!" (NLT[a]).

Planting and harvesting people to eternal life is so much more joy-filled than the cleanest house. It's better than having a coffee table dust-free without a speck of any pretend relative on it. Joy awaits us when we spread the good news that God saves through the sacrificial death of his Son, Jesus. Now that will leave a mark.

I truly do want to leave a mark. Not one from an off-course bungee. I want to leave a joy mark on the people I meet.

The Whole Enchilada

Do you want it all? The whole enchilada? Ask! I think asking for a joyful life of glorious thrills pleases the Father. It pleases him when we want all he is willing to give. It pleases him when we thirst for him and for his blessings. It pleases him when we desire to leave a joy mark on those around us by spreading joy and by sharing the good news of the difference Christ makes in our lives. Our heavenly Father doesn't want his children to merely get by. He wants us to live a thrilling life of great joy. Yes, the whole enchilada! I guess you can wrap it in a tortilla if you want—any way you wrap it, it's the scrumptious life.

The eyes of all look to you,
    and you give them their food at the proper time.
You open your hand
    and satisfy the desires of every living thing.
The Lord is righteous in all his ways
    and loving toward all he has made.

Psalm 145:15–17

30 The Total Tote

I've never met a sixteen-year-old who is as completely gaga over tote bags as my daughter Allie. The adorably dimpled child is totally bag obsessed. Or would that be "tote-ally" bag obsessed? Allie can walk into the mall on a shoe mission and come out with three bags—and still no shoes. She now officially has more totes than she has totable stuff to tote in the totes.

She even has special bags that she uses to fold and store her bags. Bags of bags. My Allie is a tote-al bag lady! She says she uses the bags to create more space, but she and I both know she's actually a bit of a sucker for anything creatively cute with a handle on it.

And while we're talking about Allie's creative flair, let me tell you that her room is a little creatively frightening to me. Have you ever walked into a room that just screamed *garage sale*? Every wall in her room is a garage saler's paradise. An Einstein mobile dangles from her ceiling fan. What true yard sale bargain hunter wouldn't pay a pretty penny for that? And who wouldn't give top dollar for that purple lava lamp? There's also a giant Batman and Robin mosaic hanging very near the shelf of old soda pop bottles and the rubber chicken.

I know you're thinking I made that last part up, but honestly, there really is a rubber chicken hanging on the wall. That means there's at least one corner of her room that looks more like a poultry slaughterhouse than a bedroom.

There's an arrow hanging on another wall and some pasta art on another. I'm hoping she didn't use the arrow to kill any rubber chickens. Creative eclectic decorator that she is, there's even a Snickers wrapper displayed like a proud "I love my chocolate" banner. Hey, if she added a vegetable, she would have decor in every food group in the pyramid. Allie's room could be part of a complete and balanced diet—and maybe a science experiment in a couple of places. Maybe that's why Einstein is half smiling from that mobile.

To be perfectly honest, though, all her original art pieces hanging on those walls? I wouldn't let those go in a garage sale for any amount of money. Those are masterpieces.

The Science of It All

Interesting masterpieces turn up in the most bizarre places. In a rather unrelated masterpiece, Kaley and I were eating ice cream with chocolate shell on it a few nights ago. Mine had an interesting art effect happening that I'm sure Allie could've turned into a creative wall-hanging. But it was too delicious to sacrifice. Not to mention she would've had quite the challenge on her hands with the melting effect. More science.

Ice cream with chocolate shell is more than just yummy dessert. It's even more science. I thought mine was pretty; then Kaley showed me hers and said, "Ooh look, the shell made a little archy thing from the ice cream scoop to the side of the bowl."

I looked, and it really was pretty impressive. I said, "Woah, it's a 'stalag-side.' "

Kaley said, "Stalag-side? That's not a word."

I said, "Well, it's not a stalactite and it's not a stalagmite—it's stuck to the side: stalag-*side.*"

She said, "Okay, but it's still not a word. That's totally made up."

I quickly argued back, "Hey, every word is totally made up."

And then I decided I would write about the word. As soon as it's in print—voilà! It's officially a word, right? That left me feeling entirely too creatively powerful.

Creatively All-Powerful

Of course, I'll only feel creatively powerful as long as I don't compare myself to the creatively all-powerful God. Did I really speak a word into existence? The word jury is still out on that one. But God did speak the world into existence. Everything. He said "let there be" and there just plain *was.* And it was good.

It's good to remember that we serve an all-powerful God. The same all-powerful God who created everything we see is the God who calls us to be holy as he is holy. The good news is that in his all-powerful creativity, he's the one who does the sanctifying. First Thessalonians 5:23–24 says, "May God himself, the God of peace, sanctify you through and through. May your whole spirit, soul and body be kept blameless at the coming of our Lord Jesus Christ. The one who calls you is faithful and he will do it." *He* does it all by his amazing power! He does the calling; he does the sanctifying.

The power to live a holy life can only come from him. That's another reason it comforts and encourages us when we dwell on the indescribable power of our God. We need to hang on to thoughts of his power to make us holy. Hang on like a stalagmite-tite-side!

Holy How-Tos

How do we hang on to holiness? How do we become holy at all? We need to remind ourselves often that actually, we don't. We can do our part to invite holy living. But we can't become holy in and of ourselves any more than the temple could make itself holy in the Old Testament. What was it that made the temple a holy place? It was the fact that the holy, holy, holy God dwelt there. So what is it that makes us holy? Holiness happens in our lives only as the all-powerful holy God dwells there. First Corinthians 3:16 says, "Do you not know that you are the temple of God and that the Spirit of God dwells in you?" (NKJV).

What's startlingly magnificent is that indwelling us is his desire. Jesus said in John 14:15–17, "If you love me, you will do as I command. Then I will ask the Father to send you the Holy Spirit who will help you and always be with you. The Spirit will show you what is true. The people of this world cannot accept the Spirit, because they don't see or know him. But you know the Spirit, who is with you and will keep on living in you" (CEV). The all-powerful, holy God will keep on living in us by his Spirit!

Do you continually desire holiness? True holiness comes from a tight, intimate connection to him, recognizing that he indwells you and that he has all power to help you live a holy life. It happens as he becomes your greatest desire and part of your every thought. Now there's a thought totally worthy of toting around—no need for a bag.

Though if you do find yourself in need of a bag, be sure to check in with Allie.

> Father, I desire that they also whom You gave Me may be with Me where I am, that they may behold My glory which You have given Me; for You loved Me before the foundation of the world. O righteous Father! The World has not known You, but I have known You; and these have known that You sent Me. And I have declared to them Your name, and will declare it, that the love with which You loved Me may be in them, and I in them.
>
> John 17:24–26 NKJV

Part 7

"For it is written: 'Be holy, because I am holy' "

31

Help for the Purse-Impaired

I clean my purse out every time I need to. Okay, I clean my purse out every time I'm shamed into it. As soon as someone refers to it as "the dirt bag," I'm usually on top of the cleanup within a week or two.

I have friends who are the polar opposite. They're purse organization fixaters. Can a person be overorganized when it comes to purse arranging? How would she know? Maybe these would be some signs to watch for.

Top Ten Signs You've Overorganized Your Purse

1. Your purse has fixed file folders
2. They're color coded, significance rated, system cataloged, regulation indexed, and cross referenced
3. You carry a label maker in your purse
4. Everything in your purse has been labeled with your label maker
5. Even your label maker is labeled with a label made by your label maker
6. Your chewing gums are in alphabetical order and arranged in subcategories of longest lasting flavor

7. You carry a specially designed tilt-proof purse to reduce the chances of tousling
8. You have separate coin purses for your pennies, nickels, dimes, and quarters
9. You sort those pennies, nickels, dimes, and quarters in order of circulation date
10. Your specially organized Day-Timer has highlighted tabs marking the appointments with your purse therapist

I would consider anyone who invests more time tidying her purse than she does *showering* a good candidate for purse overmanagement therapy. If she takes her purse in the shower with her, she may be a good candidate for a purse organization intervention. Are there support groups and twelve-step programs for the purse-impaired?

Then again, I would never be the one to make a judgment call on any purse-tidying obsession. We've already established that I could in fact use a little more compulsive cleaning behavior in the purse area. I can't even keep mine in order for a day or two.

A few more cleaning compulsions around my house wouldn't necessarily be a bad thing either. Even the sofa gets messy. There's always something strange on that sofa. A shoe with no mate, a handful of candy wrappers, yesterday's mail, day before yesterday's mail, half of a doggie chew toy—yes, quite a variety of unexpected things on the sofa. Not to mention *in* the sofa. And, boy, do we need a new one.

We need a new sofa for a couple of reasons. First, we're a wrestle-on-the-couch kind of family. It's like WWF on a smaller, sofa-sized scale. My teen boys are six-footers so it was only a few months of wrestling before the couch lost a round or two and started making a loud popping sound every time we sit on it. Hey, if I'd wanted a crunchy couch, I would've left the kids' potato chips in there, thank you very much. It makes me think of breakfast every time I sit. *Snap, crackle, pop.* I sat down the other day and I was just sure I heard my spine crackle. Scary.

Couched in Mystery

Even scarier is the second reason we need a new sofa. My sofa is a lot like my big yellow chair, only with cultures. With five kids, I shudder to think of all the fermenting Pepsi, pizza sauce, Ramen residue, and old milk that lies within (although the milk is more likely closer to cottage cheese by now). It's full of toxic liquid teenager solutions. I don't even want to know what kind of juices I'm sitting on. Whatever is in there, it's couched in mystery. Come to think of it, maybe it's good that the sofa makes that popping sound. It's probably drowning out the *squish*.

I've done a sofa-check, and any way you look at it, it's past time to burn this thing. I have to do a life-check regularly, too, to make sure I get rid of anything squishy. Sitting on something unholy? That's worse than sitting on a fermenting sofa. When Peter says, "For it is written: 'Be holy, because I am holy,'" he's quoting from Leviticus 11:44–45 and 19:2. The holiness of God is not something new. He has always been holy. The more we understand about our holy God, the more we find ourselves pursuing the holy life. And as we understand more about him, we understand all the more how deeply he despises sin. Wink our sin away? Not a holy God. Habakkuk 1:13 says, "Your eyes are too pure to look on evil; you cannot tolerate wrong."

Is It Crying Time?

He never thinks our sin is cute. In his holiness, he never dismisses it as "no big deal." We need to continually be reminded to think as he does about our sin. It should break our hearts as it does his. Sometimes we need to cry. It's not a bad thing to be brought to tears over our sin. It's our way of agreeing with God how hateful unholiness is.

What is the last thing that touched you so deeply you were brought to tears? Maybe it's been awhile since you've cried. Does it take watching *Little House on the Prairie* to induce your weeping (any episode where Charles Ingalls cries will do it for most of us)? Does it require an *Extreme Home Makeover: Home Edition* marathon to bring you to tears? It's sad when a TV show can move us to tears, yet we become somewhat insensitive to our sin. Really and truly, is there anything that should grieve us more than our sin?

Our heavenly Father never becomes callous to sin. Let's make sure we don't either. We can continue to rejoice, too, that because of the most gracious love of God, we can be made clean—forgiven. It's better than the newest, cleanest, top-of-the-line designer couch. Maybe not so much a couch as a "love seat."

As for my petri dish of a sofa, I'm not sure we'll ever get rid of the teenager juices and their various spores without giving up and burning the thing. That sofa makes my eyes water after I sit on it for more than twenty minutes. I wonder if there's an onion in there.

> As a follower of the Lord, I order you to stop living like stupid, godless people. Their minds are in the dark, and they are stubborn and ignorant and have missed out on the life that comes from God. They no longer have any feelings about what is right, and they are so greedy that they do all kinds of indecent things. But that isn't what you were

> taught about Jesus Christ. He is the truth, and you heard about him and learned about him. You were told that your foolish desires will destroy you and that you must give up your old way of life with all its bad habits. Let the Spirit change your way of thinking and make you into a new person. You were created to be like God, and so you must please him and be truly holy.
>
> Ephesians 4:17–24 CEV

---

32 My Purse Runneth Over

Does your purse ever get too full to handle? You already know I've been known to snap a strap or two. If only I didn't have those tendencies to overload. I lose more good purse straps that way.

I once tried to juggle my overflowing purse after it blew a strap. I gave the belly of the purse too hard a squeeze and watched in dread as it blew the lid off my ivory beige liquid makeup, spewing it out of the top like a purse-shaped foundation fountain. Trying to wrangle in a broken purse that's spewing makeup down the sides must look a lot like greased pig wrestling. My foundation has all those slippery moisturizing emollients—the ones just this side of extra oily blubber. It no doubt has more lubricant than the pistons of my minivan. Greasy kid stuff is . . . well . . . *kid stuff* in comparison. It was a purse-sized oil-spill disaster.

When you consider the fact that my extra-greasy foundation is probably a couple of bucks per squirt, it was a bit of a financial disaster too. That stuff is beige gold. At two bucks a shot, too many gushers could keep my kids out of college.

I've fought any inclination to over-squeeze ever since. As a matter of fact, anytime I see anyone else squeezing an overloaded purse, I have to fight the urge to dive into the nearest bunkerlike shelter, yelling, "Take cover—she's gonna blow!"

Caught in the Clutches

It's one thing to struggle with a purse you've overloaded to the point of the death of its handle. But what happens when you can't hold on to it because in reality it has no handle? What happens when your purse goes strapless?

We call it a clutch, and it's always a cute purse choice. But when you think about it, how wise is it? I can never decide exactly what I'm supposed to do with a clutch when I'm at a buffet. Trying to juggle it with a plate of food never works. What are you supposed to do with a clutch in those kinds of situations? Squinch it into your armpit? Clinch it between your teeth? Pinch it between your knees?

By the end of an evening with a clutch, you've had to hold on to it so long you have to pry your fingers off one by one. Now that *is* a clutch.

But a clutch is more than just a purse without a strap. Do trials and difficulties have you in their clutches? Did you know that you can walk in holiness and live in victory despite the circumstances?

Holiness will be the purifying result of suffering when we allow the Lord to use it that way in our lives. But it inspires a tough question: Am I still willing to beg God to make me more holy—to *pursue* holiness with every ounce of passion I have—even if it means that trials will come into my life? Not that we ever want to ask for difficulties or that we have to particularly enjoy them, but can we come to the place where we can, on some level, welcome those struggles so that we can welcome his holiness? Tough one!

Are you ready to ask yourself the "willingness" question: Am I willing to trade my comfort for a struggle if that will make me holy? Can I still passionately pursue holiness with that in mind?

The Lesson of the Overindulged Amoeba

My husband mentioned in one of his sermons that researchers at the University of California at Berkeley did an experiment that involved—strange though it sounds—indulging an amoeba.[1] They put this particularly blessed amoeba in what would amount to amoeba heaven. It was a perfectly stress-free environment. No amoeba taxes, no stressful amoeba job, no amoeba children to put through college. The researchers made sure the amoeba had the ideal temperature, had exactly the right amount of moisture, and had all its favorite foods in just the right amounts. We're talking *amoeba spa* here.

I'm picturing the amoeba in its microscopic La-Z-Boy with its tiny remote control flicking through its several hundred cable channels. I can imagine it flipping through its favorite magazines, popping pizza rolls and bon bons. This was one pampered, one-celled critter, wanting for nothing.

Wouldn't you think he'd be the fattest, happiest amoeba who ever . . . well . . . who ever did whatever amoebas do? If an amoeba could purr, surely it did. And yet, guess what it did instead of purring.

It died!

The little guy was comforted to death. It's an amoeba point to consider. Not that an amoeba has any points. But it's certainly an aspect of struggles and challenges to mull over.

Struggles and the Pursuit of Holiness

Difficulties are certainly no fun, and some present more challenges than others. But it's good to keep in mind that a life without any challenging requirements—a life with no struggles to overcome—would be a life without the victories and polish trials bring. It's a life that has little reward in the way of accomplishing a demanding task or overcoming a tough obstacle.

When we respond to our challenges in the right way, they drive us to our knees. Our struggles really can encourage our holy pursuit. The Father can even use those trials to discipline us, as only a loving father does, in the way of holiness. Hebrews 12:10–11 says, "Our fathers disciplined us for a little while as they thought best; but God disciplines us for our good, that we may share in his holiness. No discipline seems pleasant at the time, but painful. Later on, however, it produces a harvest of righteousness and peace for those who have been trained by it." Notice the harvest that discipline produces. Righteousness!

Second Corinthians 4:17 tells us that "our light and momentary troubles are achieving for us an eternal glory that far outweighs them all." We need to let our troubles inspire us to become more like Jesus, to let them refine our faith, deepen our commitment, and inspire us in our pursuit of holiness.

Leading up to 1 Peter 1:13–16, the focus passage of this book, we read these words from Peter, inspired by the Holy Spirit of God: "In this you greatly rejoice, though now for a little while, if need be, you have been grieved by various trials, that the genuineness of your faith, being much more precious than gold that perishes, though it is tested by fire, may be found to praise, honor, and glory at the revelation of Jesus Christ" (vv. 6–7 NKJV). Those "various trials" are faith-testers. They allow us to see what flows out when we're squeezed.

What flows out of you when you're squeezed? Is it holiness?

O Lord, may others see holiness flowing out every time we're squeezed! Lord, may it be praise!

Squeezing out holiness. Now that would be the best makeup of all!

The Lord is my shepherd; I shall not want.
He maketh me to lie down in green pastures:
he leadeth me beside the still waters.
He restoreth my soul:
he leadeth me in the paths of righteousness
for his name's sake.
Yea, though I walk
through the valley of the shadow of death,
I will fear no evil:
for thou art with me;
thy rod and thy staff
they comfort me.

Thou preparest a table before me
in the presence of mine enemies:
thou anointest my head with oil;
my cup runneth over.
Surely goodness and mercy shall follow me
all the days of my life:
and I will dwell in the house of the Lord
for ever.

Psalm 23 KJV

33 Tugging at Your Purse Strings

What happens when you fall in love with a purse you can't afford? Have you ever felt an exceptionally cute purse pulling at your heartstrings and pulling at your purse strings at the same time? Is it pulling your strings, or is it a little more like yanking your chain? It's a little emotional either way.

I do try to save my chain-yanking and biggest emotional responses for bigger issues than purses. I try. In all honesty, the "bigger issues" I choose for my emotional responses are still pretty embarrassing. I hate it, for instance, when I have a loud and uncalled-for emotional response when I find out someone ate the last Ding Dong. Then I hate it when I'm forced into a different kind of emotional response after remembering that I was the one who ate it—and adding insult to injury, I'm supposed to be on a diet.

Other issues that evoke emotional responses (not in any particular order) would include any wedding, a delightfully semi-decadent sale event, a funeral, a new mall, a graduation, and in the biggest response category, anything amazing or embarrassingly un-amazing my children might do.

Relatedly, absolutely anytime one of my children does something spiritually significant, you can count on floods of tears. Floods. I realize I am a blessed woman. I get to have those significant heartstrings experiences on a regular basis. My kids are 14, 16, 17, 19, and 21 as of this writing. Just seeing them in worship blesses my heart in a joy-filled emotional response of the most tear-filled variety.

Tear Generators

Would you like to take a peek at one of my blessed tear triggers? My oldest son is a church music major in college. Andrew writes the most amazing songs from a transparent heart—so many of them full of thoughtful and glorious praise. He wrote a song called "Hearts On Fire" that includes this verse:

> Our hearts are set on fire from heaven
> So sing aloud, sing all creation
> Our God is great to be praised
> Breathe in the smell of sweet redemption
> He'll open up a new dimension
> Of love, our Savior
> So sing, and dance, and pursue romance
> With the One most worthy of all our hearts can give[1]

Oh, how that brings laughter to my heart! Not the fake kind of laughter you might find in the last scene of a *Murder She Wrote* episode. No, the laughter that comes with the deepest, most celebrative heartfelt tears. It's even much more than the blessing of witnessing my son's sweet worship. It's the emotional blessing of being led into worship myself.

Recognizing God's holiness opens up our hearts to worship just that way. Psalm 138:2 says, "I will bow down toward your holy temple and will praise your name." He is the only one who is worthy of our praise. The Andy Rhea take on that praise tells us in the last verse of "Hearts On Fire" that as the sons and daughters of Zion, we can stand up. We know the name we can forever call on—the name, says the song, "that brings kings to their knees."

Kneeling Before the King of Kings

His holiness does bring kings to their knees. We worship as we're brought to our knees as well. And we worship as we love with all our hearts the one most worthy—our King of kings.

What is the reason our focal passage gives for our calling to be holy? We are called to be holy because he is holy! We've seen that *holy* means "set apart." His holiness is set apart in a different way than ours. Ours is a pursuit of righteous living. His is a state of being, set apart from any other definition of holiness. His is a "holy holiness."

The logical response to his "holy holiness" is worship. Because he is holy, we must worship him. Psalm 29:2 says, "Worship the Lord in the splendor of his holiness" (Psalm 29:2 NLT[b]).

Worship happens when I stop the pride of thinking about all I can do. That doesn't inspire worship at all. Worship happens when I stop thinking about how low and pitiful I am. That doesn't inspire worship either. Real worship begins at the place I stop thinking of self at all and place my focus on the God who deserves all my reverent adoration and praise. Thoughts of self go on the altar, and the holy God takes his rightful place as the center of attention and honor.

Singing his praises. Offering ourselves. Bowing before his greatness. Being completely taken aback—utterly awed at his holiness. We worship as we think about his holiness. His is the most blazing holiness—he's never had a speck of wrong. Not a speck. What can we do but adore and praise the only one who is truly holy?

Think about his holiness and remember his amazing love for you. He treasures you so much that his thoughts never stray from you. Worship that Savior. Adore him in praise. Bow your heart and mind and all you are to him. He deserves your worship. And you are built to adore him.

No Strings Attached

We're to be set apart too. Once we've given our lives to the holy Lord—no strings attached—those lives should look different. We should look like the one to whom we now belong. Holiness defines the new me. It defines the new you. Our desire should be to live the kind of holy lives that will glorify him. We glorify him by becoming more like him. And he is holy. Every step we make toward holiness is a spiritually significant event. I wonder if our spiritually significant worship just might bring a happy tear to the eye of the God who so loves his children.

As for my children, I'll keep working on crying more tears of joy over their spiritual successes than I cry tears of exasperation over their Ding Dong consumption—or mine, for that matter. Don't worry, the Ding Dong thing is just a joke. It's my playful way of yanking your chain.

> I will exalt you, my God the King;
>   I will praise your name for ever and ever.
> Every day I will praise you
>   and extol your name for ever and ever.
> Great is the Lord and most worthy of praise;
>   his greatness no one can fathom.
> One generation will commend your works to another;
>   they will tell of your mighty acts.

They will speak of the glorious splendor of your majesty,
  and I will meditate on your wonderful works.
They will tell of the power of your awesome works,
  and I will proclaim your great deeds.
They will celebrate your abundant goodness
  and joyfully sing of your righteousness. . . .
My mouth will speak in praise of the LORD.
  Let every creature praise his holy name
  for ever and ever.

Psalm 145:1–7, 21

34 What's in Your Wallet?

I was digging through my purse the other day, desperately seeking a gift card I just knew was in there. I remembered putting the gift card in my wallet, but it was nowhere to be found. It was a card redeemable at an adorable little coffee shop, so I was determined to find the thing.

It took awhile to realize that it had slipped out of my wallet and was lost in the vast jungled recesses of the densest spaces of undergrowth in my purse. Lost. Then came the disconcerting realization that I was going to have to stick my hand in there. I wondered if it was even safe. What if there were snakes? Do they respond to "*um-gah-wah*"?

It's a Jungle in There

I probably spend too much time pondering what a purse is made of on the outside. Leather, vinyl, fabric, canvas? Paper or plastic? Aluminum or titanium, maybe? Animal, vegetable, or mineral? Fringe, fur, or sequins—gold, frankincense, or myrrh—the bottom line is that it's out there in the open and it's not nearly as important as what's hidden on the inside. And I can hardly make myself talk about the bottom line on the bottom lining. Just the thought makes this native excessively restless.

If that coffee shop wasn't so cute and their coffee so tasty, there's no way I would've stuck my hand in the dark places of that purse. But a gift card to a shop that's cute and has the tastiest coffee too? That's treasure. I knew I had to go in.

I was forced to wade through several used tissues. That was creepy—especially since I'm not sure they were mine. I got a minor paper cut from a concealed grocery list. For a minute there I thought I was going to need that snakebite kit after all. I knew it was going to take awhile to wash off the grit of that exfoliating scrub I found spilled in there. Quicksand.

Before it was over I had some major lint, grit, and goo under my fingernails. Even that didn't stop my purse safari. Is it okay if I say that I'm a little impressed with my own fortitude over that one? That's because I really do hate it when I get gunk under my fingernails.

It was, however, all very worth it. I finally found the coffee shop card treasure. It was definitely a "Eureka!" gold-mine kind of moment. And let me tell you, that little treasure bought some mighty tasty mocha.

Digging for Gold

My purse is often like a gold mine. To dig for gold, you have to get dirty. Worse than purse lint, grit, and goo under the fingernails. I've never seen gold straight out of a mine, but I'm guessing it doesn't come out shaped in a charming little necklace or a gorgeous dinner ring. It's more likely covered with grimey grit and goo—lint drastically multiplied. Goldminers get all that slime under their fingernails, poor things. They must hate that. Yet they do it because there's treasure there.

Our holiness is treasure that we may need to dig for. Yet guess what the digging requires. Surrender! Bizarre, isn't it? We don't even have to hate it!

Our instruction is "be holy, because I am holy." It doesn't say to try to be holy. It doesn't say "compared to the average Joe Sinner, you are to be holy." It doesn't even say, "It's a good idea if you are holy." No, it's a must. It's the Romans 12:1–2 kind of sacrifice. We looked at that passage in chapter 17. Take another look in a different version: "So brothers and sisters, since God has shown us great mercy, I beg you to offer your lives as a living sacrifice to him. Your offering must be only for God and pleasing to him, which is the spiritual way for you to worship. Do not change yourselves to be like the people of this world, but be changed within by a new way of thinking. Then you will be able to decide what God wants for you; you will know what is good and pleasing to him and what is perfect" (NCV[a]).

Without thinking, we can try to substitute other things for holiness. Sometimes it's busyness. We think that if we fill our day full enough, accomplish enough, work enough, have a to-do list that's long enough, then that will please God enough. But he doesn't demand our busyness. He demands our holiness. There's no substitute.

All or Nothing

It's an all *sacrifice. You're holy, or you're not.* Jesus said in Matthew 5:48, "Be perfect, therefore, as your heavenly Father is perfect." What makes the difference? What does the Lord want? I'll tell you. He wants all of you. Every part. Holding nothing back.

We looked at what Jesus said in Matthew 22:37 in chapter 17 as well. When he said to "love the Lord your God with all your heart, all your soul, and all your mind" (NLT[b]), he was asking us to surrender all. He longs for us to come to him in complete surrender. Surrender of absolutely everything. Every burden of the past, every dream for the future, and everything in between.

In Matthew, Mark, and Luke we're told of a woman who came to Jesus with her all. She brought a very expensive perfume. A few drops and everyone would've been sufficiently impressed. But she wasn't out to impress. She gave all with abandon. And not just the perfume. She gave herself. Luke 7:37–38 tells us, "She brought an alabaster jar of perfume, and as she stood behind him at his feet weeping, she began to wet his feet with her tears. Then she wiped them with her hair, kissed them and poured perfume on them." Her tears, her service, her worship—her past, present, and future were clearly on the altar, a gift for the Savior.

How did the Savior respond? He made her whole. He gave her the forgiveness she so desperately wanted and needed. He changed her life.

We are called to that same surrender. Are we as desperate as the woman with the expensive perfume? Are we ready to pray, "Lord, I'm sick of trying to do this myself. I need you. I surrender all. Anything and everything—it's yours!"

Inside Treasure

Girlfriends, it's very true that what's on the outside is not nearly as important as what's hidden on the inside. On the outside, those people watching the woman with the alabaster jar still saw the sinful woman who had walked in. On the inside, the moment she surrendered, Jesus forgave her and made her new. She had a treasured "Eureka" kind of moment that she is still experiencing to this very day.

Surrender will set you apart. Second Corinthians 6:17 says, "Therefore come out from them and be separate, says the Lord." And living in holy surrender will make your life a treasure to your heavenly Father. What could be sweeter than that? There's nothing! Not even mocha.

> So then, any of you who does not forsake [renounce, surrender claim to, give up, say good-bye to] all that he has cannot be My disciple. Salt is good, an excellent thing, but if salt has lost its strength and has become saltless [insipid, flat], how shall its saltness be restored? It is fit neither for the land nor for the manure heap; men throw it away. He who has ears to hear, let him listen and consider and comprehend by hearing!
>
> Luke 14:33–35 AMP

35 A Purse-onal Challenge—from My Bag to Yours

Several weeks ago I had to spend an entire day canceling credit cards, getting a new driver's license, trying to piece my calendar back together—all those pain-in-the-neck panic moves we have to make when our purse is stolen.

I asked all my friends to start praying. And boy, are they good, because as soon as they started praying, my purse turned up at home tucked away in a remote place in my laundry room. So does that mean my friends are such good pray-ers that angels must've been immediately dispatched to fly over, snatch my purse from the clutches of the evil purse-pilferers, then set it gingerly down in my laundry room?

Either way, I was totally relieved. Of course, I was totally humiliated at the same time. I had filed a police report, for Pete's sake. I was *so sure* someone had taken it!

Anytime I'm feeling "so sure," I hope I'll remember the crow-eating moment of having to call the police on myself and asking them to fill out a "total idiot" report. And I'm hoping that crow is at least relatively low in calories. I had a major helping.

Certainly, my purse was never lost to God. He probably wondered why I was in such a state over a bag of lint and old tissues and that huge handful of receipts I'll never need anyway. But he never lost sight of it. And one thing I can truly be "so sure" of is that I am not lost to him either. As a matter of fact, he has never lost sight of me.

A Grace Surprise

You'll never believe what happened after I lost sight of my purse, though. I had gone to the police station to file the report, then to the license bureau to get a new drivers' license. A couple of hours later I was picking my kids up from school when I noticed flashing lights in my rearview mirror. I thought, "Man, this is just not my day."

The officer came to my window, and as I was handing him my new, hot-off-the-presses license, I noticed he was the very same officer who took my report! What are the odds? I asked him what was up and he said my tags were expired. How could I have missed that? I handed him my license again so he could write up my ticket. There was no arguing with tags that had been expired for two whole months!

In the meantime, I could tell it was all clicking in the officer's mind that I was the lady with the earlier "purse incident." He obviously felt sorry for me as he waved my license back at me. "Just so you know they're expired," he said.

It was total purse mercy! The purse incident won me some major ticket grace. Then I found out later that the purse had been misplaced, not stolen (unless, of course, the angels really did fetch it back)! Isn't that sort of sad, weird, happy, unjust, and hilarious all at the same time? I know grace is always undeserved, but in this situation the ticket mercy seemed doubly undeserved. I had broken the law, then got a pass on the ticket because of a stolen purse that in the end I found out hadn't really been stolen at all. Is there such a thing as "undeserved, undeserved grace"?

When I think of grace, my mental dictionary almost always turns to a page where "undeserved favor" is inked in as the best definition. Grace is something good that comes to someone who hasn't earned it.

The Most Gracious Grace

But the grace of God is more than that. It's something gloriously wonderful coming to someone who has earned the exact awful opposite. Joseph showed God's kind of grace when he met up with the brothers who had tried to murder him, then sold him into what they knew would be a miserable life of slavery and mistreatment. They had stolen his family, his father, and the good life from him, and they deserved the worst punishment. Joseph was in just the position to dole out that punishment. They deserved the worst. But what did Joseph give them? He gave them the best. He showed them true grace.

I am one of those brothers. Not just in the purse/ticket grace encounter, but in an eternal encounter with the holy Father. He was in the position to punish me in the worst way. I had broken the law and earned the punishment even more completely and convincingly than I had the ticket. But what has he given me? Grace! The best!

The Father who shows me grace has the same grace for you. He longs to show you grace because of his deep love for you. He treasures you—you are his delight. It's his love for you that prompted salvation.

In case I've failed to make it clear in the chapters leading up to this last one, let me say that our salvation depends on our holiness. But we desperately need to understand some essential points regarding that holiness. We need to first understand completely that while we should always strive to live holy, even the best believers—those you never see stray—can't earn salvation through their own personal holiness. Living a perfect life isn't going to get anyone to heaven in any kind of handbag, because, in fact, no one can live a perfect life. We then need to understand completely that the personal holiness we must have to experience a right relationship with a holy God only comes through Jesus Christ.

Hebrews 10:10 says that "we have been made holy through the sacrifice of the body of Jesus Christ once for all."

The Impossible Is Possible

If you've never surrendered your life to your heavenly Father through the Savior Jesus, this next section is just for you. There's not a person on this planet who doesn't need the Savior. Since sin entered the world in the Garden of Eden, we've all been separated from our holy God. Not the good kind of separated. It's the kind of separated that makes it impossible to have a right relationship—without a speck of hope of becoming holy on our own so that we can have that relationship with our holy God.

But our God is a God of the impossible. And it's his great love for us that inspired the impossible. He has never, ever lost sight of you. "God demonstrates his own love for us in this: While we were still sinners, Christ died for us" (Romans 5:8). Jesus came to live the only sinless life ever lived. "He never sinned, nor ever deceived anyone" (1 Peter 2:22 NLT[b]). He lived a perfectly holy life, then he died a sacrificial death on the cross to pay our sin penalty. Galatians 4:4–6 says, "But when the time was right, God sent his Son, and a woman gave birth to him. His Son obeyed the Law, so he could set us free from the Law, and we could become God's children. Now that we are his children, God has sent the Spirit of his Son into our hearts. And his Spirit tells us that God is our Father" (CEV).

The law mentioned there? We couldn't keep it. As a matter of fact, it points out our unholiness all the more. Romans 3:20 says, "Therefore no one will be declared righteous in his sight by observing the law; rather, through the law we become conscious of sin."

When Jesus died on the cross, he took the punishment for every sin you've ever committed. He substituted your guilt for his holiness. When you surrender to him, you are declared to be perfectly righteous in the eyes of God. Romans 3:22 tells us that "this righteousness from God comes through faith in Jesus Christ to all who believe."

Three days after Jesus died, he rose from the dead. He has all power over sin and death and has already won the victory. If you will ask him to forgive your sin and come into your life, and if you will surrender control to him, he will forgive. You can trust the promise of Romans 10:13: "Everyone who calls on the name of the Lord will be saved." You call, he saves!

Hear His Call!

If you've ever tried to achieve holiness on your own, I know I don't need to tell you what a frustrating prospect that is. Are you ready to trust Christ? Are you ready to quit running your frustrated life yourself? Girlfriend, it's no accident that you've been brought to this place in this book at this time. There are no accidents with God. This is sort of "page one" in his plan for you. If you're ready to trade the frustrated, empty life for a life of purpose—the life of holiness he's calling you to—surrender to his plan for you. You can pray something like this:

> Lord, I'm frustrated and I'm tired of struggling to do the right thing in my own strength. I'm keenly aware that it's not going to work. I know that I've sinned. I've broken your laws. I'm about as far from your holy perfection as anyone can be. Would you please show me your grace and forgive me? I believe you died on the cross to pay for everything wrong I've ever done. I believe you rose again, victorious over sin and death. I'm amazed that, in your grace, it's your desire to forgive me and to make me holy. I trust you right now to forgive every sin. Thank you for forgiving me. Thank you for loving me. I give you my life, Lord—every part.

Lord, may I use every day of life I have left in pursuing your goals for me and in pursuing your holiness. Thank you for saving me. In Jesus' name, Amen.

If you just prayed that prayer for the first time, you are a new person! Let me be the first to welcome you into this grand life of great adventure. It's an adventure that leads us right up to the gates of heaven—it's faith in Christ's saving power that results in a glorious eternal reward. If you just changed your eternal destiny from hell in a hand basket to heaven in a handbag, so to speak, would you let someone know what's going on in your life? We're going to spend eternity together! Might as well get to know each other here, right? Let a solid believer help you as you get started in your new walk with Christ.

Even after we're saved, our pursuit of holiness continues. Our holiness is not like the Father's blazing holiness. He never has to pursue. He simply *is.* But ours is a continuing process. As we thirst for righteousness, he satisfies. Matthew 5:6 says, "Blessed are those who hunger and thirst for righteousness, for they will be filled." And as he fills, we thirst for his holiness all the more.

The Continuing Pursuit

It's my desire that the thirst for holiness will continue in the most intense way. That's the pursuit! And what an amazing pursuit it's been through this book! I thank you very sincerely, my friends, for pursuing him with me through these pages. I'm praying for you and for myself, that our pursuit won't end with the last page of this book.

O Lord, may we continue to pursue holiness—all glory to the magnificent YOU. Thank you for every little word throughout this book that you've used to draw us closer to you and closer to your holiness. May we be inspired to keep up the holy pursuit with everything we've got!

Okay, girls, let's take the thought of holy pursuit with us everywhere we go! Hey, if we made a pocket-sized edition of this book that we could carry with us in our purses, would it be a "pocket pocketbook book"? Purse book or no purse book, let's purse-sist in this heavenly, holy purse-suit—that's our purse-onal challenge! And that's my purse-onal word on it—from my bag to yours.

> But now a righteousness from God, apart from law, has been made known, to which the Law and the Prophets testify. This righteousness from God comes through faith in Jesus Christ to all who believe. There is no difference, for all have sinned and fall short of the glory of God, and are justified freely by his grace through the redemption that came by Christ Jesus. God presented him as a sacrifice of atonement, through faith in his blood. He did this to demonstrate his justice, because in his forbearance he had left the sins committed beforehand unpunished—he did it to demonstrate his justice at the present time, so as to be just and the one who justifies those who have faith in Jesus.
>
> Romans 3:21–26

Notes

Chapter 7

1. "Amazing Grace," words by John Newton, circa 1772.

Chapter 22

1. Andrew Murray, *Deeper Christian Life* (n.p.: Fleming H. Revell, 1895). Public domain. From Christian Classics Ethereal Library, www.ccel.org./ccel/murray/deeper.html.

Chapter 29

1. Thoro Harris, "All That Thrills My Soul Is Jesus," 1931.
2. Author unknown, "Joy Is the Flag Flown High."

Chapter 32

1. Christopher Peterson, Steven Maier, Martin Seligman, "Optimism and Bypass Surgery," in *Learned Helplessness: A Theory for the Age of Personal Control* (New York: Oxford Univ. Press, 1993). Accessed on PreachingToday.com.

Chapter 33

1. "Hearts On Fire," words and music by Andy Rhea, 2007. Used by permission. Hear the song at purevolume.com/andyrhea.

Discussion Guide

Learning about "Purse-onal" Holiness . . . and Going to Heaven in a Handbag!

Would you like to have a holier life—a life that pleases your heavenly Father? If you're turning to this discussion guide for your own personal study time, that's wonderful. I think you'll find it easily adjusts to provide a personal application or two as you pursue holy living. Skip the "Opening It Up" prompts and bag a little extra food-for-thought by diving right into the chapter questions. There may be a few group-focused questions, but they're easily tweakable to fit your personal reflection time.

If you're picking up this discussion guide for group discussion, well—what could be more fun and fruitful than learning the *Purse-suit of Holiness* with a group of girlfriends? Grab your favorite bag and get ready for a grand purse-uit!

Notes for the Discussion Leader

Taking a group with you as you pursue purse-onal holiness? Spectacular! This discussion guide should be just the ticket to give you hints and helps as you seek to guide women in applying some truths from God's Word about holiness—what it means and how we can have it. How glorious it is when women can set a higher goal than merely reading a book. The higher goal? Getting personal, making it real, taking it to heart. Holiness in the most God-pleasing, heart-touching way!

The Purse-uit of Holiness is a journey through 1 Peter 1:13–16. Isn't it magnificent that God can change us in such dramatic, life-altering ways as we look at his Word? Watching women change right before your eyes, to the glory of God—could it get any sweeter? We'll be looking at the 1 Peter passage phrase by phrase. There are five chapters for every phrase and seven sections in all, plus an introduction.

If you would like to plan an eight-week study, you can take one section per week and add a session for the introduction. If you're able to take it a little slower, you'll find more opportunities for sharing more deeply. A chapter per week would be ideal, though you may find some folks are a little reluctant to make a 36-week commitment. Happily, anyone should be able to jump in at any time during the study. And also happily, there's really no wrong way to take your group on the *Purse-uit of Holiness*. You'll likely find a schedule that will perfectly fit your needs and your group's needs.

The questions in this guide are personal reflection questions designed to help us think about and fruitfully process what we've seen in God's Word. Each chapter will begin with an "Opening It Up" discussion starter designed to help women loosen up and laugh. Sometimes sharing on a surface level can break down barriers and free group members to later share on a deeper, more significant level. Have an answer or story ready for the kickoff in case, as the leader, you need to "open up the opener," so to speak. Many of the openers have some sort of award, trophy, or certificate. You can also add these to those weeks where one is not mentioned, if you would like. For a real hoot, put together (or ask a helper to put together) a homemade award for the best story. You'll be surprised when you see how much the group looks forward to those "Opening It Up" awards. If you take snapshots of the recipients and their awards each week, you can display them all in a hilarious remembrance at your last *Purse-uit of Holiness* group meeting.

As the discussion leader, you'll need to find that tricky balance between sharing enough of yourself to allow your group to trust you, and sharing so much that the discussion becomes "all about you." If you have a close friend in the group, it's a great idea to make yourself accountable to her and ask her to tell you honestly if you're hitting that balance well.

I would encourage you to make transparency your goal. If you will be real—even if you struggle—your group will most often respect your genuineness and will feel freer to share their own struggles as they come up.

What You'll Need to Do Each Week

Encourage your group to read the assigned chapter or chapters before the group meeting, but let them know that even if they get behind in reading, they won't feel out of place coming to the discussion meetings. Reminders through phone calls or emails are great. You can divvy up those duties or ask one of your group members if she would consider being a contact person. Even with a contact person, as group leader, it's great to check in on your group whenever you can. Ask each woman how you may pray for her.

As you're going through the week's assigned reading, make a few notes or observations you would like to point out or comment on during that week's discussion time. If the Lord teaches you something poignant, confronts you on an issue or deeply moves you in some way, openly share that with your group.

May I also encourage you to make a commitment to pray for each of your group members every week? What life-changing power there is in prayer!

After you've completed the assigned reading and prayed for your group, look over the discussion questions. Be ready to offer some answers if the discussion needs a little charge—but again, be careful not to monopolize the chat time.

It's always fun, though certainly not mandatory, to have some snacks to offer. You can call for volunteers or put something together yourself. Doesn't chocolate almost always speak to women in a profound way? I've heard it said that good chocolates are like shoes. You can never have just one.

Discussion Group Rules

You'll want to set some ground rules for the group from the very first meeting. Here are some suggestions:

- Personal information shared within the group does not leave the group. Remind each other regularly that everyone should be able to freely share and know that no one in the group will ever betray a confidence.

- If someone shares a need or asks for prayer during a meeting, a volunteer should immediately stop and pray for that need. Just a few sentences will be perfect.
- Don't allow cutting remarks or unkind comments to anyone in the group or about anyone outside the group. Uplifting, positive words only.
- Likewise, never correct anyone in front of the group. Belittling or embarrassing someone into changing their behavior rarely works. If confrontation needs to happen, it should happen in private and it should be done in love.
- If someone says something contrary to God's Word, however, let her know you respect her opinion, but also let her know, in love, what the Bible does say. God's truth needs to be our bottom line on every issue and every group discussion should reflect that.

Prayers for You!

Thank you again for taking on the role of discussion leader. You're making a difference in the kingdom! Now, may I pray for you?

> Father, thank you for the discussion leader's availability to be used by you to touch the lives of women. I ask that you would bless her in the most marvelous way for her sacrifice of service. Lord, let her find joy in this journey that absolutely surprises her. May she come to know those in her group in a deeper way. May she see the lives of women be changed by your power right before her very eyes. Would you please bring exactly the right women into her group? If there are any who don't know you in the most personal way, would you even now be drawing them to yourself?

I ask that you would grant the discussion leader great wisdom from you, insight into your Word, and sacrificial, Jesus-kind of love for each woman in her group. Knit hearts together as only you can do. Move and work in the lives of women in whatever way will bring you the most glory. Oh Lord, would you please take the leader, the group, and all of us to a holier life with you! In Jesus' name, Amen.

Discussion Guide

Introduction: It's in the Bag! *"Prepare your minds for action"*

Opening It Up: As you "open it up," share times when you've found something surprising when you "opened it up"—your purse, that is. Anything unexpected ever jump out when you opened it up? Who might win the Biggest Surprise in a Handbag Award?

1. Look at 1 Peter 1:13–16 again. As you've read through the introduction of the book and as you read God's Word, have you made any observations about the holiness of God and the holiness of his people?
2. Where should your own holiness come from? Where does *growing* in holiness fit in?
3. Are you ready to prepare your mind for action? Are you ready to think clearly? What do you think that might require from you? Pray through the prayer at the end of the introduction. And get ready for a hot holiness pursuit!

Part 1: "Be self-controlled"

Chapter 1: A Walk-in Purse

Opening It Up: Share closet stories and decide who should win the title Closet Purse-aholic. Time to come out of the closet!

1. According to 2 Peter 1:3, from where do we get what we need for living the life of holiness? How much of what we need is provided?
2. Would you like to know your holy God better? What happens as we know God better?
3. Do you have room to grow in the life of holiness? Are you ready to pursue that growth? Where might self-control fit in and what might it require of you?

Chapter 2: Pocketbook Power

Opening It Up: Who is brave enough to share the biggest problem area encountered when swimsuit shopping? Funny stories?

1. How does self-control relate to spiritual exercise? According to this chapter, how can we build holiness muscle? What specific kinds of "spiritual crunches" might it take?
2. Are you giving your spiritual fitness as much attention as (or more than) you give your physical fitness? What kind of exercises do you think might be required for you to get spiritually fit? Are you ready to start the fitness routine?
3. What kind of life do you think would be the result of ignoring these spiritual exercises? What kind of life do you think would be the result of being diligent in these spiritual exercises?

Chapter 3: Purpose in the Purse

Opening It Up: Who is willing to enter the Most Disturbing Purse Item contest? Vote on the winner and award her something comically appropriate—like a package of wet wipes or a car deodorizer with the word "car" marked out and replaced with "purse."

1. Have you ever gotten frustrated in your attempts to live a holy life? What do you think is the source of that frustration?
2. According to this chapter, self-control is not so much about gritting our teeth and determining to do better as it is about surrendering to the Holy Spirit and retraining our thinking and responses. In what practical ways can we surrender and retrain?
3. Are there some concrete steps you're willing to take in giving God's Word a place of importance in your life? How do you think growing in the area of studying God's Word will impact your pursuit of holiness? Why?

Chapter 4: Hole in One?

Opening It Up: Award the Fuzzy Tootsie Prize to the person who can pull something extra furry out of her purse. Anyone have a "fuzzy surprise" purse story to tell?

1. What are some practical ways we can become more self-controlled in getting rid of sin? Name some ways we can stay alert to those areas of sin that sneak into our lives.
2. Can you think of a time in your past when you lugged around some sneaky sins that weighed you down? How did you get free? How did you feel once you did get free?

3. Are there any sins right now that you're lugging around? Do a little life check. As the Holy Spirit shows you things you need to confess, confess them on the spot.

Chapter 5: Polka-dot Purse

Opening It Up: Ever find something moldy or mushy growing in your purse? Mold check time! Who might win the It's Alive! Award?

1. Do you ever feel like a total failure in living the life of holiness? Where do self-control and discipline fit in at that point?
2. When we fall, what does Proverbs 24:16 tell us we should do?
3. How would you compare and contrast our failures in living a life of holiness with the mercy of God? How should his mercy affect our pursuit?

Part 2: *"Set your hope fully on the grace to be given you when Jesus Christ is revealed"*

Chapter 6: A Purse Verse

Opening It Up: In an approximate inventory, who has the fewest items in her purse? Three cheers for the winner of the Got Her Bag Together Award for the most organized purse!

1. Think about all the ways God meets your needs. Can you name at least ten? Are you growing in your dependence on him, counting on him to meet your every need?

2. In heaven, our Father will meet our needs in the most glorious way. When you think about heaven, what do you imagine will be your favorite part? What does it do to your hope quotient when you ponder what heaven will be like?
3. How does the grace of God affect your hope?

Chapter 7: There's a Face in My Handbag

Opening It Up: Who would win the Face-Off Prize for the most unique make-up item? The funniest item?

1. Where does 1 Peter 1:13 tell us to set our hope? And according to Titus 2:11–12, how does that affect our holiness in the here and now?
2. How do you think holding on to guilt over sin we've already confessed affects the pursuit of living a holy life? What would you tell a girlfriend who came to you struggling with that kind of guilt? If you're the one lugging around that kind of guilt, are you ready to embrace God's grace and let go of the guilt?
3. How complete is God's grace in covering every sin? How effectual is his forgiveness? Celebrate his amazing grace!

Chapter 8: Oh Purse Feathers!

Opening It Up: Who has the wildest "outrageously huge" or "ridiculously small" purse—or purse tale?

1. What does 1 John 2:28 instruct us to do? What are some practical ways we can do that and what do you think the results will be?

2. What kind of "readying" do you think it takes to be ready for Jesus' coming? How does that look when it's lived out?
3. What are the qualities of a life that is waiting expectantly for his return? Do you see any of those in your life? Are any missing?

Chapter 9: I'm Packin' Heat—There's a Blow-dryer in Here

Opening It Up: Anyone eligible for the Save It for a Rainy Day Award with a great story about getting caught in the rain? Who's had something ruined in a storm?

1. Ever think about how much you don't know? How about what we will know when we see Jesus face to face?
2. Have you thought about how thoroughly the Father knows you? And how thoroughly he loves you? How does knowing those two things inspire you to live a holy life?
3. How would you describe a hope that is "fixed"?

Chapter 10: Nurse the Purse

Opening It Up: Does your purse take on a different feel when you travel? Who has had a bit of Purse-911 on a trip? Any other purse emergencies? Anything you've forgotten?

1. Look at Philippians 3:13–14. According to this chapter, what are the three kinds of things we might need to "forget"?
2. Have you ever known someone who held on to a hurt? What does bitterness do to a life in the pursuit of holiness?
3. Have you ever been one to hold on to an offense? If you're harboring bitterness right now, would you be willing to ask

the Lord to set you free from it? Pray the suggested prayer in chapter 10 and watch God work!

Part 3: *"As obedient children"*

Chapter 11: Im-purse-onator

Opening It Up: Who wins the We're Naming Names Award for the best designer knock-off? Anybody gotta Prada that's more of a Yada Yada? How about a knock-off story?

1. Read Philippians 2:9–11 and then spend some time describing the name of Jesus. Any praise breaking out? Celebrate his name!
2. What effect does bearing the name of Jesus have on our pursuit of holiness? Why is being God's child such an inspiration to live holy?
3. What does Ephesians 5:1 say should be the result of knowing we're God's children? Do you think your life lines up with this verse? Are there any areas that could use some improvement?

Chapter 12: Walk Softly and Carry a Gargantuan Purse

Opening It Up: Who has the heaviest purse? A scale and a "weigh-off" would be fun—to find out whose purse is the lightest and who is a real purse heavyweight.

1. What is our "heavy artillery," our best weaponry in spiritual battles? What does this do for us? For our thought lives?
2. Read Joshua 1:7–8. What does this say will be the result of reading, meditating on, and obeying the Word of God?

3. Are you willing to pray the prayer in this chapter? *O Lord, inspire me more and more every day to love and treasure your Word—to read it, study it, and do it!* What kind of difference does this prayer make in a life?

Chapter 13: Designer Bags

Opening It Up: What's the biggest price tag you've ever seen on a purse? Did it look like it was worth it? Who has seen the ugliest handbag with the heftiest price tag? Doing a little online purse search and printing out the web pages of the most outrageously expensive bags could be a real jaw-dropper—and a real hoot.

1. How does society generally assign a person's worth or identity? How does that compare with where you find your own personal value?
2. Have you thought lately about how much God loves you? Do you ever doubt that he could love you?
3. If you had a price tag, according to this chapter, what would be on it? What does that tell you about God's love for you? How does that translate into the way you live?

Chapter 14: Purse-onification

Opening It Up: Ever had a fake nail pop off at an inopportune moment? Ever broken a real nail at exactly the wrong time? Share your best nail stories.

1. What happens when we refuse to listen to the Lord's instructions—or we refuse to obey?

2. Has the Lord ever asked you to do something you felt you just didn't have the ability to do? How does that compare with what the Lord told the Israelites in the Deuteronomy passage discussed in chapter 14?
3. What are some practical, day-to-day ways we can listen to the Lord?

Chapter 15: In My Grandma's Handbag

Opening It Up: Can you remember the sights, smells, and sounds of your grandmother's purse? Who has the sweetest "grandma" story?

1. With this chapter in mind, think of the pursuit of holiness with an "if" attached to it, and compare and contrast it to the pursuit of holiness with a "whatever" attached to it. Which one best describes your life? Are there any "ifs" that need to become "whatevers"?
2. Do you ever find yourself pursuing blessings instead of holiness? When that happens, what can turn your life's pursuit back to holiness?
3. What difference does serving out of love instead of duty make in our pursuit?

Part 4: *"Do not conform to the evil desires you had when you lived in ignorance"*

Chapter 16: That's a Purse of a Different Color

Opening It Up: Who might win the Rainbow of Purses Award for owning the most purses in the most different colors? If you had a "mood purse," what color would it be right now?

1. How do you think a person's pursuit of holiness affects her mood? How can her pursuit affect those around her?
2. How does our own passion for holiness influence our families and friends? Can you think of someone who has been a positive influence on you? Do you think you might be a positive influence on someone else?
3. Are there any sin habits hindering your pursuit of holiness that you've yet to get rid of? Are you ready to get rid of them?

Chapter 17: This Bag is Smokin'!

Opening It Up: Is there anyone who could be dubbed Ms. Gadget of the group? Who has the most tech-filled purse? If you could invent your own purse gadget, what would it be/do?

1. Have you ever seen people who seem to love God with their hearts and souls, but not with their minds? How does that compare with the lives of those who love the Lord with everything they've got?
2. Where does changing a person's behavior start? What are some practical ways we can rewire our thinking?
3. Are there still old ways of thinking buzzing around in your brain, affecting your walk in Christ in all the wrong ways? If so, are you ready to rewire?

Chapter 18: Purse Burps—and Other Embarrassing Discombobulations

Opening It Up: Are there any purses in your group that have more of a diaper bag personality? Who can pull everything but a baby from her purse?

1. How do we learn what action the Lord wants from us, as Ephesians 5:17 tells us to do? What should be the result of such learning?
2. Have you ever heard someone excusing sin, labeling it as "I'm just tired" or "It's just a little white lie"? Have you ever been the person doing the excusing?
3. What does 1 John 1:8–9 tell us about sin and what we need to do with it? How often do you think we need to do that? What needs to change in the way you've been dealing with your own sin?

Chapter 19: I Found My Purse, Now Where Are My Keys?

Opening It Up: Who has the most intense story of a lost purse? How about lost keys? How many times a month do you misplace your purse or your keys? Who wins the distinction of being the group's Biggest Loser?

1. Do you ever find yourself feeling like you're not accomplishing anything spiritually? Do you think setting reachable goals can change a person's pursuit of holiness? If you haven't set any goals, do you think mapping them out would make a difference for you?
2. According to this chapter, what is the one goal we all have in common? What are some specific goals that should fall under this main goal?
3. Are you ready to go through the goal suggestions in chapter 19 and make some detailed lists of solid actions you can take to help meet your main goal? As you consider adding activities and projects to your schedule, do you think it would make a difference if you consistently asked yourself

the question, "Does this help me hit one of the goals that will make me look more like Jesus?"

Chapter 20: Purse on a Rope

Opening It Up: Wouldn't a "make your own shower purse" project be fun? Who has other ideas for handy-dandy purse projects?

1. How do you fuel holiness? How do you stop fueling unholiness?
2. Are there any areas from which you need to *run?* Is there a certain kind of book, magazine, TV program, movie, person, or situation you need to flee? Are you willing to make that sacrifice for the sake of holiness?
3. Have you ever considered having an accountability partner? Have you considered asking someone to pray for you in a specific area of your pursuit of holiness? What kind of difference could that make?

Part 5: *"But just as he who called you is holy"*

Chapter 21: Never Purse-nickety

Opening It Up: What's your most annoying, mindless habit? Any drummers, tappers, or fingernail clickers? How about whistlers, hummers, or knuckle-poppers? Ready for an annoying habit talent show?

1. Why do you think it's easier to see the faults in others than the ones in ourselves? How do Matthew 7:3–5 and 1 Corinthians 13:5 apply to how we view faults?

2. How important to our heavenly Father is our sacrificial love for others? If you had to give yourself a grade on how well you're loving others, what would it be? Has the Lord ever pricked your heart about how you treat people?
3. Has God ever pricked your heart about who you spend time with? What kind of influence does your circle of friends have on your pursuit of holiness?

Chapter 22: Pick Yourself Up by Your Own Purse Straps

Opening It Up: What's the worst high-fiber snack you've ever tried? What snack food wins the I'd Rather Eat My Purse Award?

1. Have you ever let sin go too long without confessing and getting rid of it? What effect does that have on our personal holiness? On our dispositions? On other aspects of our lives?
2. Reread 1 John 1:9 in the Amplified version. Describe the feeling of finally getting rid of a sin you've been hanging on to for too long.
3. Discuss each of the four steps of confession in chapter 22. Have you ever prayed through each one? What difference does this confession make in your life?

Chapter 23: The Purse Universe

Opening It Up: Who wins the This Will Curl Your Hair Award for the scariest hair story? Anyone have a tale of a good hairdo gone bad?

1. Have you given any thought lately to how God has put you together? How he has fashioned you with gifts and talents?

Name some ways you're using your God-given gifts and talents to serve.

2. Reread 1 Peter 4:11. What do you think this verse might imply about God's provision for our service?
3. When you read the question in this chapter, "Do you want an easy life or a holy and satisfied one?" did it make you stop and think? What are your heart's desires right now?

Chapter 24: It's a Landfill in a Bag

Opening It Up: Compare all the lotions and creams in the group. Who wins the Most Skin Grease in a Bag Prize for the biggest lotion collection in one purse? Who guarantees her lotion works the best? Is there a Biggest Softy in your group?

1. What does it mean to thirst truly for the Lord? Do you thirst on a regular basis? List some things that could keep us from thirsting for him.
2. Look at Psalm 63:1–3 again. Do you think this passage gives us some practical ways we can become thirsty for the heavenly Father? If so, what are they?
3. How do "living thirsty" and "living holy" compare and connect?

Chapter 25: Purse-severe!

Opening It Up: Whose purse has the tastiest center? Anyone have a handbag with a chocolaty center? Bigger question: Is she willing to share?

1. Compare and contrast living a life of self-righteousness with living a life of true holiness.

2. Do you think it's relatively easy to start thinking that a life of holiness is just for your pastor or the leaders of the church? If so, why?
3. What are some practical things we can do to make sure we're living on the right side of that comparison? How can we purse-severe?

Part 6: *"So be holy in all you do"*

Chapter 26: The Bottomless Purse

Opening It Up: Is there a winner of the most Perfectly Packed Purse Award? Who is the Mary Poppins of the group—"practically perfect in every way"?

1. Have you ever wanted to take the easy route to holiness or settle for being "mostly" holy?
2. Read 2 Corinthians 7:1 in the New King James Version. What do you think "perfecting holiness" means? How does that translate into our walk with Christ?
3. Where does the "want to" to live holy come from? Where else do we look to inspire a desire to live right? How are those ways different from God's way?

Chapter 27: Purse Your Lips

Opening It Up: Pull out all the lipsticks from your purses and read the color names. Any woman's personality match up with the name of her lipstick?

1. According to this chapter, what happens when we come face to face with the holiness of God? Has this ever happened to you?
2. What was Isaiah's response after his unclean lips were touched with the burning coal in Isaiah 6:1–8? How does that relate to us and our responses?
3. Why do you think so many people are not really interested in holiness?

Chapter 28: Get Some Purse-pective

Opening It Up: Who might win the Purse-o-saurus Award for the oldest handbag? Does anyone have a vintage find? Is anyone willing to admit to having a "stale style" bag in their closet?

1. Describe the life of a person who is taking control and deciding to live a holy life on her own. How does this differ from a Holy Spirit-controlled life?
2. What does it mean in 2 Corinthians 10:4–5 when we're told to "capture every thought"? List some everyday ways to do that.
3. How does your Christian walk measure up to the list? Are there any changes you need to make? If so, are you ready to make them?

Chapter 29: Dis-purse-ing the Joy

Opening It Up: Whose purse is stuffed tighter than an enchilada? Any zippers stretched to the max? Who wins the I Need a Bigger Bag Award?

1. When Jesus is "more than life" to us, what characteristics do our lives take on? What characteristics do you see in your life? Is joyfulness one of them?
2. Why do you think there is such joy in a righteous and holy walk, even when circumstances are difficult?
3. Name some joyful people in your life. Does their joy often spill over to you? Do you think you have the kind of joy that spills over to others?

Chapter 30: The Total Tote

Opening It Up: Who has tote bags, tote bags, and more tote bags? Do you collect a tote bag at every women's conference and special event? Who could tote in a tote full of totes?

1. Have you ever spent time contemplating the indescribable power of our God? When we ponder his power, what effect do you think that has on our trust in his ability to empower us to live holy?
2. According to this chapter, how do we hang on to holiness?
3. 1 Corinthians 3:16 gives us the secret to holy living. How does this verse apply to you?

Part 7: *"For it is written: 'Be holy, because I am holy'"*

Chapter 31: Help for the Purse-Impaired

Opening It Up: Is your purse compulsively tidy, or do you find a few strange items in there from time to time? Think of other places where odd items are often discovered. What's the strangest thing you've ever found in, under, or around your sofa?

1. Do you think it's true that the more we understand about our holy God, the more we will find ourselves pursuing holiness? Why or why not?
2. Describe what our holy God thinks about our sin, according to the Bible. Do you think our sin saddens us as much as it saddens him?
3. Can you think of a time when you were so saddened about your sin that it brought you to tears? If so, how was your life different after you dried those tears? Why?

Chapter 32: My Purse Runneth Over

Opening It Up: Compare your "beige gold" foundation products. The Thanks for the Foundational Truths Certificate goes to the one who has the best make-up tip!

1. How do you think trials and difficulties affect our pursuit of holiness? What kind of effect should they have?
2. Have you ever asked yourself the questions presented in this chapter? Perhaps you should ask them now: "Am I still willing to beg God to make me more holy—to pursue holiness with every ounce of passion I have—even if it means that trials will come into my life? Am I willing to trade my comfort for a struggle if that will make me holy? Can I still pursue holiness with great passion with that in mind?"
3. Can you name any good things that have come about in your life as a result of trials you've faced?

Chapter 33: Tugging at Your Purse Strings

Opening It Up: Have you ever cried over spilled milk? Is there an emotional response you've experienced that was so much bigger than the situation called for that you were embarrassed?

1. What does it mean when we talk about our God who is "set apart"? What does it mean for a believer to be set apart?
2. What do you think inspires worship? What hinders it?
3. Read through Psalm 145:1–7, 21 from your Bible or from the end of the chapter. Does the passage inspire a sweet time of praise and worship for you? What is your response?

Chapter 34: What's in Your Wallet?

Opening It Up: Who could be crowned The Gift Card Queen for the biggest stash of gift cards in one purse? Should the prize be a *gift card*?

1. According to this chapter, what does digging for holiness "treasure" require? What does a life look like when a person is truly digging for holiness?
2. Have you ever seen someone who seemed to be substituting something else for the pursuit of holiness? What did they appear to be substituting? What was the result in that person's life?
3. To what do Romans 12:1–2 and Matthew 22:37 call us? How does applying these passages change a life?

Chapter 35: A Purse-onal Challenge—from My Bag to Yours

Opening It Up: Has it been a hoot of a purse-uit? What has been your favorite moment through the "Opening It Up" sections of this *Purse-uit of Holiness*? Which story or contest purse-onally gave you the biggest laugh-charge?

1. When did you first get in on the salvation discussed in this chapter? How has your life changed? If you've yet to surrender your life to Jesus, would you consider praying the suggested prayer in the "Hear His Call" section?
2. Describe the connection between our salvation and our holiness. Where do we get a righteous standing before God? How does that influence our holy pursuit?
3. How has the Lord used this book and this discussion time to impact your life? Will you determine to not let the last page of the book or the last meeting of your discussion group be the end of your pursuit of holiness? What can you do to continue the pursuit?

Rhonda Rhea is a humor columist and has written hundreds of articles for *HomeLife, Today's Christian Woman, Marriage Partnership, ParentLife,* and dozens more publications. Also a radio personality, she is a frequent guest of Focus on the Family's *Weekend Magazine* and *Audio Journal.* The author of several books, including *I'm Dreaming of Some White Chocolate* and *High Heels in High Places.* Rhonda and her husband, Richie, live in Troy, Missouri, with their five children. She invites you to visit her website at www.rhondarhea.org.